THE ECONOMIC THEORY OF REPRESENTATIVE GOVERNMENT

ALDINE TREATISES IN MODERN ECONOMICS

Edited by
Harry G. Johnson
University of Chicago and
London School of Economics

THE ECONOMIC THEORY OF REPRESENTATIVE GOVERNMENT

Albert Breton

University of Toronto

ALDINE PUBLISHING COMPANY
CHICAGO

ABOUT THE AUTHOR

Albert Breton is Professor of Economics at the University of Toronto. He received his Ph.D. in Economics from Columbia University and has been associated with the University of Montreal, the University of Louvain, the London School of Economics, and Harvard University. Dr. Breton was also Director of Research from 1956-65 for The Social Research Group in Montreal. His articles have been widely published in the major U.S. and Canadian journals.

Copyright © 1974 by Albert Breton

First published 1974 by
Aldine Publishing Company
529 South Wabash Avenue
Chicago, Illinois 60605

ISBN 0-202-06064-0
Library of Congress Catalog Number 73-75704

Printed in the United States of America

To Margot

There is nothing sacred about the conventional boundaries of economics; if the cycle were meteorological in origin, economists would branch out in that direction, just as in our day a political theory of fiscal policy is necessary if one is to understand empirical economic phenomena.

P. A. SAMUELSON

Contents

IV.   RESOURCE ALLOCATION IN THE
PUBLIC SECTOR

V.   APPENDIX

Foreword

The purpose of the Aldine Treatises in Modern Economics is to enable authorities in a particular field of economics, and experts on a particular problem, to make their knowledge available to others in the form they find easiest and most convenient. Our intention is to free them from an insistence on complete coverage of a conventionally defined subject, which deters many leading economists from writing a book instead of a series of articles or induces them to suppress originality for the sake of orthodoxy, and from an obligation to produce a standard number of pages, which encourages the submergence of judgment of relevance in a pudding of irrelevant detail. The Aldine Treatises seek to encourage good economists to say what they want to say to their fellow economists, in as little or as much space as they consider necessary to the purpose.

Economics used to be taught under the name of "political economy," along with government and political philosophy. In pursuit of the status of "economic science," it has in modern times separated itself from that association and has attempted to tackle problems of public policy and public finance by the use of the tools of economics alone on the assumption that these were purely economic problems set by a government that existed only to serve the public good. Gradually, however, and particularly in the past fifteen years or so, a number of economic theorists have come to realize that this assumption is far too naive to be useful, and that government must instead be understood as one of the major economic institutions of society and one that behaves like more familiar economic institutions—the household, the firm—though the markets it confronts are markets for policies and for votes rather than for goods and services. They have accordingly set to work to apply the key concepts of economics—demand and supply, and maximization subject to a budget constraint or to a constellation of demand and cost curves—to the explanation of governmental behavior.

Albert Breton is one of the leading younger scholars in this new field of study. He has had the advantage of personal acquaintance with other established scholars, as well as with their works. He has also had the advantage of having lived and taught not only in the United States—the origin of scholarly concern about the economic theory of representative government—but in Canada, the United Kingdom, and Belgium. Hence he has been able to test the central propositions of the emerging theory against observation of different systems of government, and to refine them where they conflicted with or failed to illuminate the facts.

This book reflects the fruits of a decade of Breton's thought, study, and teaching of the subject. The analysis is cast in a simple demand, supply, and demand-supply-equilibrium framework. But to construct that framework, it is necessary to explain why government exists and what it provides that the ordinary economic institutions of the competitive marketplace cannot provide. The answer is found in the concepts of "public" and of "non-private" goods; and much simplification and clarification is achieved by conceiving of government as offering "policies" with respect to the output of these goods, rather than the goods themselves—for example, "law and order" rather than policemen and their equipment, law courts, and jails. It is also necessary to go beyond the rather naive concept of political parties as competing for votes with rival policies at election times, to a concept of political activity as continuous in time and of the governing party as subject to constraints on its behavior while in office. In addition, political theories of government seldom if ever pay attention to the influence on the governmental process that may be exercised by bureaus.

The subject may seem a rather peripheral one to academic and other workaday economists. But such economists frequently are puzzled by the failure or refusal of governments to adopt what seem to them the only possible reasonable policy; and it is not really intellectually satisfactory to blame the stupidity or venality of politicians for behavior that is both persistent and, in its own terms, consistent. Breton offers an alternative and intellectually far more satisfactory explanation: that governments are behaving economically in the light of their situation in the social structure, and that their behavior can be understood and explained by the standard and well-tested principles of economic analysis.

HARRY G. JOHNSON

Acknowledgments

This small book has been many years in the making. Many parts of it have served as seminar and lecture material to university audiences in Belgium, Canada, England, and the United States. As a consequence, it is difficult or, more exactly, impossible for me to thank individually all those who by comments and criticisms have contributed to what is of value in it; but I, nevertheless, wish to express my gratitude to them as a group.

I must, however, express my thanks in a special way to Harry G. Johnson who more than anyone else over the last decade or so has encouraged me to pursue the ideas which I have put down in these pages; he has read and commented on all the drafts of this volume and on many of my earlier papers connected with it. Though he cannot be held responsible for the final product, it must be recognized that that product would have been very different without his continuing help.

My gratitude extends in a special way also to James M. Buchanan, John H. Dales, Alan T. Peacock, Anthony D. Scott, Gordon Tullock, and Ronald Wintrobe, all of whom have read an earlier draft of the book and made a large number of most helpful comments. They cannot either be held responsible for the remaining inadequacies, but all of them helped shape the finished book.

Among my students, I wish to mention David Husband, Frank Juhasz, and Clifford Walsh, who all became interested at one time or other in the subject matter of the volume and have forced me to focus on some aspects of the public sector which would have otherwise escaped me. None of them have been gone from the student world for long enough not to remember that their responsibility for my changes of mind has always been known to be limited.

I

Background and Definitions

Acknowledgment of Receipt

There are two ways in Czech to translate the word manifestation:
manifestace, when one agrees; _demonstrace_—as in the English
demonstration—when one does not. One's desire is then to prove,
to render obvious an opinion that cannot be expressed in other ways.
That is why squads of intervention or tanks of intimidation are not
very apt ways to react. The worst thing that can happen to a message
is that it will not be heard, and the most deaf are those who do not wish
to hear.

By bludgeoning, by imprisoning, by spraying, by apprehending,
by shooting, the guardians of the law are providing
the demonstrators with exactly what they want:
an acknowledgment of receipt acceptable
the world over. (Author's translation)

ROBERT ESCARPIT

1

An Introduction

1. The Background

In the last fifteen years or so economists, returning to a tradition which they had to all appearances completely abandoned, have produced a growing volume of research on the problem of collective choice. If we bear in mind that the classification of analytic and scientific work is always somewhat capricious, it is possible without doing too much violence to these writings to classify them under four major headings, to wit, the theory of public goods, the theory of democracy, the theory of decision-rules, and the theory of transaction costs.[1] It may not be intuitively obvious that all this research work has a bearing on the question of collective decisions: this may explain why each particular field of research has until now largely, but not wholly,

1. What I call the theory of public goods has historically been developed and formulated under various names: Wicksell discussed it under the heading of "A New Principle of Just Taxation" ("Ein neues Prinzip der gerechten Besteuerung"), while Samuelson labelled his discussion "The Pure Theory of Public Expenditure". As the subsequent discussion should amply emphasize, it is neither a theory of taxation, nor a theory of government expenditure; it is an existence theorem about public goods coupled with a market failure theorem.

3

lived a life of its own, unimpeded in its growth by the issues discussed in the other areas.

The theory of public goods,[2] to focus on the first body of knowledge listed above, remains, even after the courageous attempts of Buchanan and others, a theory devoid of any *decision-making mechanism*.[3] In other words, the theory is still mainly an existence theorem of welfare economics concentrating almost exclusively on the definition of equilibrium conditions, and the refinements and generalizations which have occupied researchers in more recent years have done scarcely anything to remove this crippling and fundamental emptiness. The theory, as it now stands, does not shed any light on the problems of collective choices or, to put it differently, it is still without an institutional counterpart. To say, as the theory does, that the presence of public goods in an otherwise well-behaved system is consistent with Pareto and Bergson optimality but leads to market failure is important and useful, but it is not particularly instructive about the forces that ultimately determine the allocation of resources between public and private goods. At

2.   K. Wicksell, "A New Principle of Just Taxation," in R. A. Musgrave and A. T. Peacock, *Classics in the Theory of Public Finance* (London: Macmillan & Co, 1964) pp. 72–118; P. A. Samuelson, "The Pure Theory of Public Expenditure," *Review of Economics and Statistics* (November 1954) pp. 387–89; "Diagrammatic Exposition of a Theory of Public Expenditure," ibid. (November 1955) pp. 350–56; R. A. Musgrave, *The Theory of Public Finance* (New York: McGraw Hill, 1959) Ch. 4; R. H. Strotz, "Two Propositions Related to Public Goods," *Review of Economics and Statistics*, (November 1958) pp. 329–31.

3.   J. M. Buchanan, *Public Finance in Democratic Process* (Chapel Hill: University of North Carolina Press, 1967); and especially *The Demand and Supply of Public Goods* (Chicago: Rand McNally & Co., 1968); J. S. Coleman, "Foundations for a Theory of Collective Decisions." *American Journal of Sociology* (May 1966) pp. 615–27; "The Possibility of a Social Welfare Function," *American Economic Review* (December 1966) pp. 1105–22; C. M. Tiebout, "A Pure Theory of Local Expenditures," *Journal of Political Economy* (October 1956) pp. 416–24.

the same time, there is no doubt that many private and collective decisions involve public goods (or non-private goods) and that a theory of collective choices cannot pretend that these goods do not exist.[4]

The theory of democracy,[5] on the other hand, though grounded in decision theory, does not do very much more than pay lip service to the existence of public goods.[6] The existing economic model of democracy incorporates essential institutional elements of observable democracies such as "representative" political parties, decision-rules, and one transaction cost, namely the cost of information. Furthermore individuals and political parties are assumed to pursue certain definite objectives, to

4. Except for a modification suggested in the next chapter (section 6), the best definition of public goods is still Samuelson's. He defines a public good as a good "which all enjoy in common in the sense that each individual's consumption of such a good leads to no subtraction from any other individual's consumption of that good. . . " ("The Pure Theory of Public Expenditure," p. 387). Following Samuelson, I have defined a non-private good as one "which, though not available equally to all, has the property that the amount available to one individual does not reduce that available to others by an equal amount" ("A Theory of Government Grants," *Canadian Journal of Economics and Political Science* (May 1965) pp. 175–87. I devote chapter 2 to related problems of definition.

5. A. Downs, *An Economic Theory of Democracy* (New York: Harper and Row, 1957) and "Why the Government Budget Is Too Small in a Democracy," *World Politics* (July 1960) pp. 541–63; J. Q. Wilson, "The Economy of Patronage," *Journal of Political Economy* (August 1961) pp. 369–80; J. Rothenberg, "A Model of Economic and Political Decision-Marking," in *The Public Economy of Urban Communities*, ed. J. Margolis (Baltimore: Johns Hopkins Press, 1965) pp. 1–38; R. Dorfman, "General Equilibrium with Public Goods," in *Public Economics*, ed. J. Margolis and H. Guilton (New York: St. Martin's Press, 1969).

6. H. R. Bowen, "The Interpretation of Voting in the Allocation of Economic Resources," *Quarterly Journal of Economics* (November 1943) pp. 27–48; and *Toward Social Economy* (New York: Rinehart, 1948), chapter 18, did wrestle with the problems of the relationship between voting and the supply of public goods, but his political model is too rudimentary to be treated even as a prologue to a theory of democracy.

make decisions, and to interact with one another within a well-specified and more or less realistic institutional framework. But the theory does not incorporate the essential "conflict-full" element of joint consumption which is an integral property of public and non-private goods. Indeed, the only constraints on the behavior of political agents in Downs' theory of democracy—and after almost fifteen years, Downs' is still the most complete and the most relevant statement of the theory that is available—come from the competition that is assumed to exist between political parties and from the limited amount of information that all political agents are assumed to have. The theory is therefore primarily a theory of how competition can work in a world where information is costly and where it is not profitable, at least for a large number of the agents, to acquire any. There is no doubt that Downs' work has greatly increased our understanding of the workings of the public sector, but it is difficult to believe, when one observes the large amount of political activity that exists in democratic societies, the large flow of political news put out by media seeking to maximize the level of their rating and/or the value of their advertising revenue and hence the attention of a large number of people, and the large number of individuals who vote, that political information exists in very small amounts.[7] At the same time, it is difficult to believe that competition between political parties can be a strong constraint on behavior when elections take place at intervals of two, four, five, or seven years, depending on the society and the particular institution one is looking at.

The introduction of public (and non-private) goods in the theory of democracy changes that theory very substantially as will be obvious in the next chapters; it does this by bringing into

7. It was suggested to me that it is probable that not a single day goes by in any given year without an election of some kind taking place in the United States.

the theory a set of constraints that crucially influences the behavior of political agents. To illustrate,—in Downs' theory politicians act so as to maximize the number of votes cast in their favor, a hypothesis which, in a modified form, I will adopt in this study; what restrains them in the things they can do to achieve that goal is political competition and nothing else. In the following chapters, we will see that public goods impose constraints on the behavior of politicians very similar to the constraint that a production function imposes on the maximization of profits by entrepreneurs supplying private goods in competitive markets. This does not mean that competition does not play any role, but it plays a role with other constraints.

What I have called the theory of decision-rules can be formulated to incorporate the concept of public goods and that of transaction costs; as it stands, however, it has not been integrated with the existence of such institutions as governments and political parties—the essential building blocks of the theory of democracy—though Buchanan and Tullock have gone part of the way in bridging that gap.[8] A central feature of the theory of decision-rules is the assumption of direct personal interaction: the essential characteristic of this assumption is that decisions about whether a good (public, non-private, or private) should be provided or not and in what quantities are reached directly through the interaction of the individuals concerned and are not mediated through an institution such as a representative or a government. To put it differently, direct personal interaction implies that the preferences of individuals are satisfied through face-to-face bargaining, logrolling or vote-

8. K. Arrow, *Social Choice and Individual Values* (New York: John Wiley, 1963); D. Black, *The Theory of Committees and Elections* (Cambridge: Cambridge University Press 1958); J. M. Buchanan and G. Tullock, *The Calculus of Consent* (Ann Arbor; University of Michigan Press 1962).

trading (with or without monetary side payments), issue-voting (to be distinguished from voting for representatives), and/or any other schemes in which citizens are involved in deciding directly on the supply of goods. The mechanism is therefore significantly different from the one underlying the theory of democracy in which the preferences of individuals are satisfied at one remove through representatives, as is most certainly the dominant case in practice.[9]

Furthermore, very few of the strong features of decision-rules have been incorporated into the existing economic theory of democracy. The fact, for example, that any rule, other than unanimity, makes it possible for the governing party to neglect the demands of some members of the electorate has been recognized but not made an integral and essential part of the theory of the workings of the public sector.

Not only is the theory of decision-rules consistent with what we know about transaction and bargaining costs, but our understanding of the behavior of these costs has been greatly enhanced by the more recent developments of that theory.[10] Basically transaction costs are the costs—measured in money and time—of engaging in a given activity. They include the costs of entering into the act of buying (or of selling) a flow of goods and services and therefore comprise, among other things, the costs of information, of preparing and policing contracts, of getting to and from the "market," of insuring against risk and uncertainty, etc.[11] Little is as yet known about these costs and in particular about their height and the way they vary with

9. Tullock has briefly discussed the question of representation in *The Politics of Bureaucracy* (Washignton D.C.; Public Affairs Press, 1965).
10. Most especially by the work of Buchanan and Tullock.
11. There is much about these costs in economic writings. The important role they play was, however, most strongly emphasized by the work of R. H. Coase. See in particular, "The Nature of the Firm," in A.E.A., *Readings in Price Theory* (Homewood, Ill.: Richard D. Irwin,

particular quantities, but economists have come to recognize that they are extremely important.

Among transaction costs one must include the cost of organizing an activity, and as a consequence these costs play a crucial role in determining the form of existing institutional arrangements as well as the type of rules, regulations, and decision-mechanisms societies adopt. It is therefore not surprising that they play an important role in Downs' theory of democracy and in Buchanan and Tullock's theory of decision-rules. They certainly have a role to play in any well-developed theory of representative government.

In the formulation of the theory of decision-making and resource allocation that I will suggest in this study, each of the four theories mentioned above has a role to play. It is true that all of them have been modified, sometimes drastically, so as to be more easily integrated with the others and with other concepts, but each one has been of extreme importance in the development of the central model.

2. The Purpose

Even if anchored in the works of others, this study has a different purpose and objective than those appear to have. Its central purpose is to provide a theory capable of explaining the measured and observed pattern of government expenditures and taxation for the democratic countries for which data is available. Though the theory could presumably be extended to cover those situations where expenditures are financed by increasing the national debt, the deficit in the balance of payments, and/or the supply of money, the model developed in the next chapters

---

1952) pp. 331–51; and "The Problem of Social Cost," *The Journal of Law and Economics* (October 1960) pp. 1–44.

assumes that all expenditures are financed by tax revenues. The assumption simplifies the task without, it is hoped, unduly restricting the applicability of the model.

There are three points related to the objective of the study that need emphasis. First, the theory applies to decision-making at the level of government and is therefore not a general theory of collective choice. There are indeed many areas where collective decisions are made other than in the public or government sector, and this study, even if it may shed light on some, though by no means on all, of these decisions, is not written with that aim in mind. Second, in the often mischievous but still useful language of methodological writings, this is a positive and not a normative study. Positive theory—as distinguished from positive empirical research—is treacherous, since value judgements and preconceptions have a way of creeping into the analysis mostly by dimming one's perception of some relevant aspects of reality. For that reason should the reader discover unannounced normative propositions or statements, he is asked to be indulgent.[12] The theory, however, contains a number of normative implications which will eventually have to be made explicit, but that is a task for the future. Third, the model is static and not dynamic. At some points in the analysis, the recognition of the existence of an election period, that is, of an interval of some positive length between election days, and its integration into the analysis does impart a dynamic flavor to the discussion, but there is no getting away from the fact that the methodology used is that of statics and of comparative statics.

It has been said that even if a statical and comparative statical analysis is acceptable for the range of problems that have

12. At a few points in the text, I have indicated the nature of the normative problems posed by the theory and given hints about their solution; I warn the reader of these digressions whenever they occur.

traditionally been defined to be within the boundaries of economics, such an analysis cannot be used for issues that are political, since politics is essentially dynamic. That may indeed be the case. But it should be remembered that, beyond the fact that the meaning of the word *dynamic* is not obvious, there is the additional fact that a statics of the political process has not yet been developed and, as a consequence, declarations on these matters are adjudications on theories that do not exist. Passing judgment on the value of things to come is always a risky business!

3. The Approach

It may be useful to add a few words in this introduction on whether the theory developed in these pages is an economic theory or not. The principle of the division of labor has been intellectually approved since Adam Smith because it is known that its application leads to greater efficiency. This principle also applies when the labor is intellectual, and it is largely because of this that knowledge has been broken up into units. The resulting gains in efficiency have been large enough to compensate for the cost of these divisions.

On the other hand, what is called the demarcation of jobs—the painter will not fill a crack in the plaster because that is the mason's job; the mechanic will not repair a defective faucet because this is the plumber's job—is generally condemned because it leads to inefficiency. Superficially, however, the two phenomena—the division of labor and the demarcation of jobs—have a rough resemblance which is often pointed to by those who stand to lose from efficiency. The same applies when the jobs are intellectual research jobs, and here also the temptation exists to let an efficient division of labor become an inefficient demarcation of jobs.

The postulated institutional framework and many of the concepts used in this study have not historically been considered part of economics; the objectives, the subject matter and many of the tools, however, have. Since in a fully employed economy, the main task facing economists is that of understanding the forces that influence and determine the flow of resources as they are allocated between competing ends, this study is strictly economic. The tools used by economists to analyze resource flows are of two types: first, the tools of marginal analysis which are especially designed to study the choices and decisions of individual economic agents, and second, the tools of stability analysis intended for the study of the interaction of market supply and demand and, hence, for the analysis of the collective adjustment of the individual agents. Both types of tools are used in this study and in that sense also this study is economic in nature.

Because the institutional framework in which the decisions of individuals are made and in which the collectivity interacts is not the market but the public sector, the traditional division of labor between economics and the other social sciences is abandoned; however, because the theory of choice that I use is the one underlying all economic theory and because I am wholly and solely concerned with resource allocation and resource flows, the traditional division of labor is respected. Only a blind and bigoted adherence to job demarcation would condemn this new arrangement.

4.   The Language

In the foregoing discussion I have used the word *individual* or *agent* to refer to the basic individual unit of the model. That is not descriptive enough and, as a consequence, in the remainder of this study I will use the word *citizen*.

This term must be defined. I do not use the word to refer to an individual who carries a passport or other papers; a citizen is one who in other studies of public choice has been called the "consumer-voter." He is an individual who participates in the political process or who would if the cost of doing so were low enough. By that definition there are individuals in every country who are not legally citizens but who participate in the political process and are therefore citizens from our point of view. In addition to non-naturalized immigrants, one can point to the Cuba Lobby in the United States, to the American Lobby in Kuwait, or to the Rhodesia Lobby in Britain. (I do not mean to imply by these examples that all the members of the Cuban, American, or Rhodesian lobbies are "foreigners.")

On the other hand, there are individuals who are legally citizens of a country but who are not so by the definition adopted here. These individuals are absolute strangers to the political process; they do not and would not vote even if the cost were zero; they do not and would not engage in any political activity; they have no interest in public affairs and therefore do not talk about them; they do not influence others and do not seek to; they are politically anomic.

Often in this study I use the words *political party*, and very often when I do I distinguish between the governing and the nongoverning parties. Except when otherwise stated I use the term *governing party* to refer to the group of persons who have captured the control of the governmental or state machinery as a result of democratic elections; and I use the term *nongoverning, contending*, or *opposition party* (or parties) for the group seeking to gain (or regain) that control.[13] In societies where the

13.   This definition is substantially that of Downs in *An Economic Theory of Democracy*, except that I do not, as the discussion of chapter 7 should make clear, assign identical goals to all members of the group *as a matter of definition*.

number of parties is large, it may not be reasonable to seek to capture the apparatus of state; the only reasonable objective may be to aim to be a member of a coalition. Groups of persons seeking that objective should also be defined as political parties. For some purposes it may also be useful to include in the definition of the group of individuals seeking the control of the government, individuals who are not themselves particularly interested in control, but who are members of the group seeking control. In many cases these individuals are local leaders acting as "hobbyists" in the public sector.[14]

The rest of the language I use in this study—except for the concept of government policies and that of the institutional framework to which I devote the next two chapters—are either technical economic terms that have a well-known meaning or they are words with a fairly common and standard usage.

5. The Strategy

As I have just stated, the next chapter is devoted to the definition of government policies, and chapter 3 to the definition of the institutional framework for collective choices. The importance of chapter 2 arises partly out of the gap that exists between accounting concepts of public expenditures and the true economic concepts, and that of chapter 3 out of the determining influence of the institutional framework on all the magnitudes analyzed in this study.

These problems of definition cleared away, I move in part 2 to a discussion of the forces underlying the demand for public policies. Chapters 4 and 5 deal with these forces as they affect the individual citizen and with the nature of the citizen's

14. I am grateful to Gordon Tullock for suggesting that the definition of a political party be widened to take these possibilities into account.

participation in the political process. In chapter 6, the configuration of demand as it is revealed in the public sector is analyzed.

Part 3 deals with the problems of supply. Chapter 7 is devoted to a discussion of the hypothesis made about the behavior of politicians and political parties, while chapter 8 examines the technical constraints which bind the behavior of politicians. In chapter 9, a hypothesis about the behavior of bureaucrats is suggested and the interrelationships between politicians and bureaucrats is examined.

In part 4, the various building blocks are brought together in one model. Chapter 10 deals with the properties displayed by the model in equilibrium and chapter 11 analyzes certain comparative statical displacements from an initial equilibrium.

2

The Output of Governments

1. Introduction

Our knowledge of the public sector is so scant that we do not even have an accepted definition of the output of governments. In this chapter I suggest a definition that is consistent with and indeed inspired by the theory of public decision-making developed in subsequent chapters. Consequently, I depart from current accounting definitions but suggest a way of moving from the theoretically correct definition to the accounting ones since empirical work can only be based on the latter.

In the previous chapter I referred to public and non-private goods and implied that these were supplied by governments, though I carefully avoided saying that governments provide all the public and non-private goods in the economy or that they provide only that type of goods. There is no doubt, however, that such goods are provided by governments. How should these goods be defined? One of the tasks of this chapter is to dissociate the concepts of public and non-private goods from material objects such as battleships, lighthouses, and parks and to relate them to the much broader and more meaningful concept of public policies. Indeed, I wish to suggest that the true outputs of governments are policies and that these are the relevant objects on which to focus attention in formulating a theory of the public sector. Public policies, however, range widely from full employment to pest control, from space exploration to tariff protection, from national defense to public transportation, and from housing programs to anti-Semitism, to name but a few. One cannot hope, therefore, to enumerate all possible government policies, even if it could be shown that such an exercise had some analytical usefulness. For this reason I have chosen to develop the analysis of this chapter with the help of a few examples which I hope cover the whole range of governmental policies.

Two general procedural points should be made at the outset: the first pertains to the distinction between policy objectives and policy instruments—two concepts that I will use throughout this chapter—and the second relates to the definition of policy instruments. At a formal level, one can define a policy objective as a variable which enters the utility function of the individual members of a government's jurisdiction, while a policy instrument is one which does not.[1] Such a definition is useful but mostly in pointing out that members of society will often disagree on what is an objective and what is an instrument. This lack of agreement is at the heart of much misunderstanding about the governmental process, for if a citizen defines a policy as an instrument, while the government takes it to be an objective—or vice versa—the citizen will accuse the government of inefficiency even if by hypothesis we assume that the government acts so as to minimize the real alternative costs of achieving what it takes to be a policy objective. It is intuitively obvious—as I will demonstrate below—that treating a policy instrument as if it were an objective leads to an inefficient outcome at least

1. J. J. Polak, "International Coordination of Economic Policy," *I.M.F. Staff Papers* (July 1962) p. 151.

in terms of cost minimization. Many of the debates on in-efficiency and wastage in government rest on a disagreement as to whether a policy is an instrument or an objective.

In this study I resolve these problems by assuming that the basic objective of the governing party is the maximization of a utility function defined for a probability of reelection vari-able and for other variables that will be introduced later; indeed I assume throughout that a governing party will treat a policy as an objective if doing so will increase its utility and that otherwise it will treat that policy as an instrument. But in this chapter I am solely preoccupied with definitional questions and hence will classify policies as objectives or as instruments according to the needs of the particular problem analyzed.

The second procedural point is this: the data we possess on households and firms gives us a fairly good idea of the quantum of resources flowing through these institutions; this is not the case for governments. These latter, in addition to expenditures on goods and services—magnitudes which are recorded in the public accounts—can by legislation require their citizens to spend on goods and services sums of money they would not otherwise have spent in that fashion.[2] To put it differently, the use of legislation as a policy instrument can mean that citizens will spend a part of their income on some goods and services, while the *decision* to spend has been that of the government. For example, the government may decide that all automobiles will have side mirrors or tires meeting certain specifications or that all garbage cans will be made of plastic or that only smoke-less fuel will be used in fireplaces in private houses. If there are citizens who would not otherwise have bought these goods, the

2. The modus operandi of governments is the enactment of laws. I therefore do not use the words *legislation* and *law* in their usual sense, but restrict their meaning to cover only non-budgetary items.

government's legislation is equivalent to an increase in government expenditure *and* taxation, even if the accounting budget of the government remains unchanged. Consequently, in the following discussion, I distinguish between the *economic* and the *accounting budgets* of governments, reserving the first term for the total of government outlays *plus* the difference between what citizens buy as a result of the legislation and what they would have otherwise freely purchased or, to put it differently, plus the difference between the price of the good that citizens are forced to buy and what it is worth to them.

By the use of legislation, the government may require citizens to spend on things that they would not otherwise have purchased, but by the same token it may introduce a wedge between potential output or income and actual output. A wedge of this kind may, of course, appear as a result of ordinary spending by government, but the instruments that produce it are more often the simple enactment of a law. For example, a government may impose a tax on foreign products, or it may implement a disequilibrium price structure for railway transportation; both policies will reduce social output below what it would be possible to extract from the existing stock of resources. The difference between this potential output and what is actually produced is also a part of the economic budget of the government.

The definition of government output adopted in this study is therefore quite different from that underlying the empirical studies of the evolution of government expenditures, the comparative studies of the relative size of the government sectors between jurisdictions, the theoretical analyses of the optimal size of the public sector, and even plain, everyday discussions of the problems of social balance or imbalance, all of which share in common a definition of government expenditure that is really an accounting and not an economic concept. I hope that the definition proposed here will eventually help to clarify some of the questions raised by these studies.

2. Police Protection

The first example I will use to define one part of government output, that of police protection, is meant to illustrate the definition of such disparate policies as fire protection, sewage disposal, national defense, public transportation, outdoor and indoor recreation, weather modification, health services, as well as most of the activities which usually involve the purchase of some inputs (policy instruments) in the open market. It is not easy to give a clear and precise theoretical definition to the class of policies illustrated by police protection, but even if the boundaries of the class are fuzzy, the identification in practice would seem to be fairly simple: they are the policies that one would impute to an "allocation branch" in a government if such a branch existed.[3]

In examining police protection, it is easy, and thus would seem superfluous, to distinguish between objectives and instruments. But precisely because such a task is relatively clear cut, I will emphasize the distinction in what follows as a preparation for more difficult cases. To most individuals police protection is identified with night sticks, dogs, cars, police officers, two-way radios, helmets, truncheons, revolvers, and all the paraphernalia that goes with the profession. In this study, however, I assume that police protection is the policy objective and that the various items just listed are the factors of production or policy instruments that are used to produce police protection. I further define the policy objective as the probability that one's person and/or one's property will not be attacked

3. For a definition of the "allocation branch," see Musgrave, *The Theory of Public Finance*, chapter 1.

by criminals in such a way that when this probability increases the amount of police protection supplied increases and when the probability falls, it decreases.[4]

To conduct the analysis, I assume that the government minimizes the cost of providing a given amount of police protection—an assumption which is quite defensible once the division of policies between objectives and instruments is given, but one that has to be reinterpreted for each new classification of policies, as the following analysis will show. Suppose now that only two policy instruments are needed to produce police protection: policemen (labor) and motorcycles (capital), which, for simplicity, I take to be fully divisible. Then referring to the standard analysis of production, one can derive the efficiency conditions for the production of any given amount of police protection. For example, in figure 2.1 the government is producing (and providing) q_1, q_2, or q_3 of police protection; the number of policemen and motorcycles used to achieve the objective depends on the market price for policemen and motorcycles if the government is paying market prices and on these prices minus a tax (or plus a subsidy) if it is not paying market prices. If the relative prices were those portrayed by the slope of AA', and if the government wanted to provide q_3 of police protection, it would use EF police-officer-days and OF motorcycle-mile-days.[5]

---

4. See C. S. Shoup, *Public Finance* (Chicago: Aldine, 1969), pp. 115–118; also "Standards for Distributing a Free Government Service: Crime Prevention," *Public Finance* 19 (1964): 383–92.

5. At that point the cost $K = m_1 C + m_2 M$ is minimized subject to the production condition $q = f(C, M)$ and therefore the first-order conditions for a minimum $f_C/f_m = m_1/m_2$ are met. The amount of police protection is q, C and M are the number of policemen (in man-days) and motorcycles (in mile-days) respectively, m_1 and m_2 the market prices of C and M, $f_C = \partial f/\partial C$ and $f_m = \partial f/\partial M$. The argument can therefore be easily generalized to any number of policy instruments.

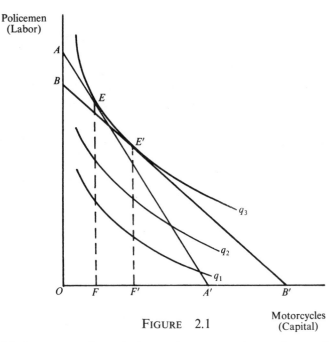

FIGURE 2.1

Motorcycles
(Capital)

If, however, the relative prices were those shown by the slope of BB' and the government still chose to provide the same amount of police protection q_3, it would use $E'F'$ of police-officer-days and OF' of motorcycle–mile–days. One should therefore expect variations in factor intensities (that is, in the use of policy instruments) in the production and provision of public policies as a result of variations in relative prices.

A decision to expand the output of police protection could, even at constant relative factor prices, also lead to a change in factor (i.e., policy instrument) ratios, depending on the shape of the expansion path. Only if the production function is linear homogeneous—that is, displays constant returns to scale—will the ratio of policy instruments used remain unchanged along the expansion path.

It is now possible to analyze the consequences of treating an instrument as if it were an objective or, to put it differently, of altering the division of policies between objectives and instruments. To proceed I assume that the governing party—for reasons which I do not wish to investigate now but which are related to the maximization of its utility function—takes both the employment of a number of police-officer-days and the provision of a certain quantity of police protection to be policy objectives. The analysis can be conducted with the help of figure 2.2. Suppose that the authorities still wish to provide q_3 of police protection, but that in addition they also want the number of police-officer-days to be OJ. This can be achieved

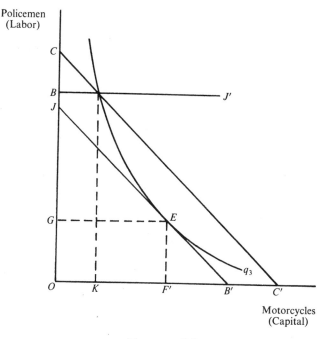

FIGURE 2.2

by reducing the number of motorcycle-mile-days from OF' to OK; at the new equilibrium, OJ of police-officer-days and OK of motorcycle-mile-days are used, and the total budget of the authorities has increased from OBB' to OCC'.

Those citizens who think that the number of police-officer-days should be not a policy objective but a simple policy instrument will call the difference in cost a waste, while those who agree with the governing party that to have OJ of police-officer-days is a proper policy objective will call the excess cost the price of achieving that objective. This case—though slightly artificial—well illustrates the conflict that can arise from the differences in tastes about policies and instruments which were mentioned earlier.

The foregoing efficiency analysis tells us how factor inputs will be combined for any level of production, but it does not tell us which level of output will be produced. To find that out we need to know something about demand conditions and about how governments react to these conditions. That is the task of the next chapters.

The policy instruments listed above are not the only ones that a government can use in providing a given amount of police protection. It can also legislate. It could, to remain with our example, require that all units under its jurisdiction build a wall around their property and that they own a large dog. Such legislation would help provide the desired police protection. Note, however, that if the government decides to provide some or all police protection in this way, the cost will not appear in the accounting budget of the government, even though the flow of resources in the economy is in fact responding to government decisions. It should be emphasized also that once policies are divided into objectives and instruments, the choice between legislation and other policy instruments will be determined by relative price considerations as long as these do not interfere with the ultimate objective of the governing party.

Suppose, for example, that given the techniques of production and the relative price of factors, it would be less expensive to provide a certain level of police protection by legislation requiring citizens to erect walls and to purchase dogs but that the fraction of the electorate (determined by the electoral system) which is relevant to the maximization of the governing party's utility function has a strong aversion to walls and to the use of dogs for that purpose. In such circumstances the governing party would not choose between legislation and other policy instruments by considering relative prices, though having decided not to use legislation, relative price considerations would presumably preside over the governing party's choice as to which of the other policy instruments to use.

The discussion of police protection illuminates an important side issue related to the analysis of government budgets. Many of the factors of production or policy instruments that enter the production of police protection are *private* goods even if the output or policy objective is itself a *public* or a *non-private* good; there is, therefore, no way of knowing whether a government will deal only in public goods short of a careful and detailed analysis of production processes and of market conditions.[6] In the above discussion, I have assumed that the government produces its own output of police protection. This, of course, need not always be the case, and if the government purchases the policy outright, as it could in the case of police protection by hiring Pinkerton's, for example, the incidence of private goods in the government's accounting budget would be very different than if the government itself produced the good, since the purchase of private goods (factors of production) would now be by the private producer and not by the government. Furthermore, the size of the accounting budget relative to that of the economic budget could be different depending

6. Private goods may enter the government budget for other reasons as we will see in chapter 8.

on whether the government's supplier was more efficient than the government in producing police protection and whether the government paid prices reflecting real economic values. If the government paid more than the alternative value of the resources used up in producing the public or non-private good, the economic budget could be smaller than the accounting one; obviously it could also be larger.

3.   Full Employment and Price Stability

Full employment and price stability, being stabilization policies, have usually been analyzed with different tools than have allocation or distribution policies. In this section I wish to suggest that even though they differ from other policies in some respects, from the point of view of decision-making at the government level, these policies should be analyzed in the way I have analyzed police protection.

To do this we must first distinguish between policy objectives and instruments. Consequently I make the assumption that full employment and price stability are policy objectives or, equivalently, that some citizens individually derive satisfaction directly from these policies and therefore that they are arguments in their utility functions. One could obviously assume that these two policies are intermediate objectives aimed at achieving maximum output, which would then be the ultimate policy objective.[7] Such an assumption is surely one that can be defended in certain contexts, but I believe it to be less useful in understanding the actual behavior of governments regarding

7.   On the hierarchical structure of policies in the theory of economic policy, see R. A. Mundell, "On the Selection of a Program of Economic Policy with an Application to the Current Situation in the United States," *Banca Nazionale del Lavoro Quarterly Review* (September 1963), pp. 262–84.

full employment and price stability than the assumption I have chosen to make in this section. Among the policy instruments, one can list debt management, fiscal and monetary policies, devaluation or appreciation of the currency, import restrictions, export subsidies, and "income-policy" aimed at influencing relative product and factor prices through moral suasion or even by direct legislation.

Given the division of policies between objectives and instruments, it is possible to relate them in the following fashion:

$$\dot{P}/P = F(V_1, V_2, \ldots, V_v; W) \qquad (2.1)$$

$$U = G(V_1, V_2, \ldots, V_v; W) \qquad (2.2)$$

where $\dot{P}/P$ is the rate of inflation—the opposite of price stability—U the level of unemployment—the opposite of employment—V_i the instrument variables, and W a vector of other unspecified variables influencing $\dot{P}/P$ and U. For some purposes it is useful to view (2.1) and (2.2) as production functions. Viewed in this way, the problem is that of combining policy instruments in the best possible way so as to produce the desired level of $\dot{P}/P$ and U, much in the way that factors of production are combined to produce police protection, motor cars, or dishwashers. It is true that the professional economist believes—and rightly so—that he is a more qualified expert of the technology of full employment and price stability than of that of police protection, motor cars, and dishwashers, but this should not hide the basic formal similarity of the structure of all these production problems.

Maximizing (2.1) subject to given levels of (2.2) yields a transformation function, which is shown as $T_m(\dot{P}/P, U) = 0$ in figure 2.3.[8] I have drawn that transformation curve convex

8. In deriving the transformation functions, I assume static expectations about price increases, that is, that the elasticity of expectations with
continued on p. 28

to the origin, but other assumptions could certainly be made since the definition of government output is not dependent on any one assumption about the shape of the transformation curve. Suppose now that because of a definite preference for a certain class of policy instruments, a new division of policies between objectives and instruments is adopted; the maximization of (2.1) subject to levels of (2.2) *and* to specified values of certain instrument variables will generate a new transformation function portrayed as $T_n(\dot{P}/P, U) = 0$ in figure 2.3. This new function is necessarily a second-best one and cannot lie bodily to the left of $T_m(\dot{P}/P, U) = 0$, since this latter function is derived without placing any restriction on the values of the instrument variables. The desired level of employment and price stability is given by the tangency of a concave-from-below indifference curve and the relevant transformation curve.

As can be easily verified from figure 2.3, one obtains a higher value of unemployment for all levels of inflation with the second-best transformation curve than one does with the best or optimal one. Again, as with police protection, those citizens who agree with the governing party in fixing some of the instrument variables at a certain level will call the value of foregone output from increased unemployment $(U_n - U_m 0)$ the price paid for satisfying this preference for operating these instruments at that level, while others will call it waste.

Let me provide an illustration of the foregoing formal argument. One instrument that is often fixed at a given specified disequilibrium level is the foreign price of domestic currency or rate of exchange. To rationalize that phenomenon, we can assume that citizens derive utility from a particular value of the

---

respect to price changes is equal to one and I neglect the existence of lags. On the elasticity of expectations, see J. R. Hicks, *Value and Capital*, 2nd ed. (Oxford: The Clarendon Press, 1946), p. 205.

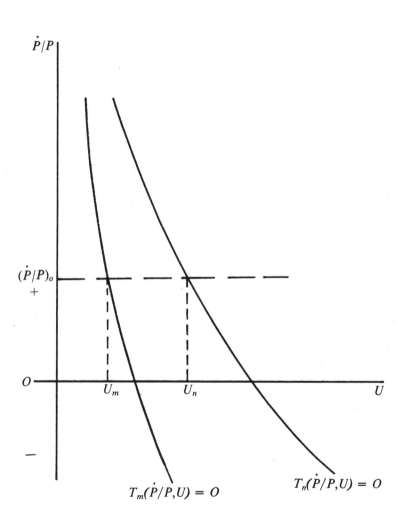

FIGURE 2.3

exchange rate; maintaining it therefore becomes a policy objective. There are many reasons why people may derive utility in this way: some people may think that the prestige of their country is linked to a given value of the foreign price of their currency; some may like to think that their government is in control of the situation and departures from a given rate indicate that it is not or has not been; and/or still others may have a preference for the distribution of income generated by an overvalued currency.

To achieve the objective of protecting the currency, governments can use one or a combination of instruments. Among the more important are: import restrictions, export subsidies, domestic deflation, exchange controls, bank or discount rate increases, and restrictions on investment abroad and on the movement of tourists. The cost of using these instruments can usually be approximated, but whether this can be done or not does not affect the argument put forward.[9] These costs are either waste or the price of achieving a given objective, depending on the point of view, or in technical language on whether the preference orderings of citizens include or exclude the policy instruments as objectives.

Finally, note that the size of the accounting and of the economic budgets will vary with the policy instruments used. For example, a budget surplus (or deficit) achieved by changes in expenditures and/or taxation will reflect itself in the accounting budget, while the use of wage and price controls will usually

9. Practically all the work on the measurement of welfare cost is relevant here. In the literature dealing specifically with exchange rate disequilibrium, one should note J. Hause, "The Welfare Costs of Disequilibrium Exchange Rates," *Journal of Political Economy* (August 1966) pp. 333–52; H. G. Johnson, "The Welfare Costs of Exchange-Rate Stabilization," *Journal of Political Economy* (October 1966) pp. 512–18; and A. O. Kruger, "Some Economic Costs of Exchange Control: The Turkish Case," ibid. (October 1966) pp. 466–80.

not have an accounting counterpart, except insofar as the machinery to implement an incomes-policy is a costly one. Indeed, variations in the choice of instruments in the pursuit of price stability and full employment are likely to be among the important contributing factors to variations in the level of the accounting budget.

4. A More Equal Distribution of Income

The logic applied in the preceding pages can be used to examine the question of achieving a more (or less) equal distribution of income, though special problems arise in this case which are not met in the analysis of other public policies. For example, governing parties are often more preoccupied with distributions over regions, trades, and other groups, than over persons. Similarly, they are often more interested in the distribution of industrial employment, manufacturing output, or other sectoral indices than with the distribution of income. One could argue that whatever objective is chosen by the governing party, the analysis of the policy pursued will not be altered since in principle all distributions can be converted into a distribution over persons and the impact of changes in sectoral indices on the distribution of income can be measured. But one cannot deny the difficulties that such exercises entail nor can one deny that it may be more useful to focus on the precise objective pursued by the governing party than to try to convert the policy into one of income redistribution.

Whatever distribution is chosen as a policy objective—income, consumption, employment, manufacturing output or any other—and whatever the units over which the redistribution is contemplated—persons, regions, professions—the fact that some redistribution is defined as a policy objective implies that some citizens have a preference for such an objective or, to put it differently, that such an objective enters their utility functions. This may occur because the welfare of others—defined as income, consumption, employment—enters the utility function of these citizens or because they hold to certain ideas or opinions about what constitutes the proper distribution of income.[10]

For purposes of normative theory, it is important to know why the welfare of one individual enters the utility function of another—compassion, commiseration, fear, apprehension—but such knowledge is not important for positive analysis since observed behavior and not changes in welfare are the concern of this last type of analysis.

The more difficult problem in the analysis of redistribution, however, arises when we focus on policy instruments. Redistribution can be achieved by transfers of money and/or by transfers of goods and services. The full meaning of the problem can only be appreciated by reflecting on the fact that properly defined and measured the supply of any public or non-private good or service at other than benefit tax-prices (namely, prices that are equal to the marginal benefits derived from public and non-private goods) automatically changes the distribution of income.[11] In view of the fact that benefit rates of taxation are in practice impossible to define, all public policies that are of a public and non-private goods variety influence the

10. Discussion of this question can be found in K. E. Boulding, "Notes on a Theory of Philanthropy," *Philanthropy and Public Policy* ed. F. G. Dickinson (New York: N.B.E.R., 1962) pp. 57–72; W. S. Vickrey, "One Economist's View of Philanthropy" ibid., pp. 31–56; S. C. Kolm, "La production optimale de justice sociale," *Economie Publique,* ed. H. Guitton (Paris: Centre National de la Recherche Scientifique, 1968) pp. 109–78; E. O. Olsen, "A Normative Theory of Transfers," *Public Choice* (Spring 1969) pp. 39–58; and H. M. Hochman and J. D. Rodgers, "Pareto Optimal Redistribution," *American Economic Review* (September 1969) pp. 542–57.

11. Strotz, "Two Propositions Related to Public Goods," *Review of Economics and Statistics* (November, 1958).

distribution of income. In a way, all of this study can be read as a contribution to the problem of valuing public output and hence as a contribution to the analysis of changes in the distribution of income. Once public output is properly valued, it will be possible to measure the extent of the redistribution achieved by the entire budget of the government—that is by taxation and expenditure policies, the last obviously defined to include exhaustive as well as non-exhaustive (i.e. transfers) expenditures.

5. Nationalism

It is sometimes said of a government that it is antisemitic, fascist, anti-American, white supremacist or that it is nationalistic. Such characterizations are surely intended to be descriptive of a broad class of policies; as such, however, they are not very useful. To be so, these epithets have to be given an operational meaning; that is, an answer must be found to the following questions: What are the policy objectives of an antisemitic government? What are those of a white supremacist government and so on for all possible characterizations. To illustrate, in the following discussion I will examine the behavior of nationalistic governments by proposing an answer to the question of what are the policy objectives pursued by nationalists.

At the outset one must distinguish between policy objectives which do not involve any significant resource flows and those which do. The actions which fall in the former class I call cultural nationalism, since they are mostly limited to flag-waving, anthem singing, chest-thumping and to the writing of historical and philosophical treatises on the greatness of one's present, but mostly of one's past. Those objectives which involve a significant flow of resources I call economic nationalism. I limit the discussion to this second type.

Without pretending to be exhaustive, it is possible to list a number of fairly specific objectives which nationalists pursue, even though they may often limit themselves to one or two of these. First, nationalists often place a value on the ownership by members of their own ethnic or national group of physical assets located in their own territory and consequently they seek to increase the fraction of the total stock of physical capital in that territory which is owned by members of their own national group.[12] Second, nationalists may try to increase the country's or region's share of industrial production in total output; this implies that these individuals derive satisfaction or utility from industrial production itself, a satisfaction which is different from that derived from the industrial products themselves.[13] For example, satisfaction is derived from steel produced in the home territory which is different from the satisfaction which is derived from consuming steel products. A third policy objective is derived from the higher value that nationalists place on "native" brains than on "foreign" brains; as a consequence they focus on the export of indigenous human capital and neglect the import of outside brains or, if they take it into account, place a low or even negative value on it. Finally, nationalists often take pride in self-sufficiency and autarky,

12.   This is the only objective which I considered when I wrote "The Economics of Nationalism," *Journal of Political Economy* (August 1964), pp. 376–86.
13.   This policy objective has been defined by H. G. Johnson in "A Theoretical Model of Economic Nationalism in New and Developing States," *Political Science Quarterly* (June 1965), pp. 169–85, and in "An Economic Theory of Protectionism, Tariff Bargaining and the Formation of Customs Unions," *Journal of Political Economy* (June 1965), pp. 256–83; see also C. A. Cooper and B. F. Massell, "Toward a General Theory of Customs Unions for Developing Countries," *Journal of Political Economy* (October 1965), pp. 461–76. In the last two of these papers, the preference for industrial production could, but need not, be a product of nationalism.

and because of this they seek to reduce the dependence of their economy on foreign markets by reducing the flow of imports.

In pursuit of one or more of these objectives, a number of policy instruments can be mobilized. Basically, there are five such instruments: (1) direct subsidies; (2) indirect subsidies which can take a number of forms ranging from tax concessions to price controls in the form of price ceilings and/or floors; (3) tariffs; (4) outright purchase of a running concern owned by foreigners or threatened by foreign ownership, an activity often called nationalization; and (5) legislation in the sense given this word in this chapter.

The marginal cost, that is, the cost of an extra unit of any one objective achieved through the tariff, is

$$K_t = \sum_i t_i(P_i\varepsilon_i + C_i\eta_i) \qquad (2.3)$$

where t_i is the proportional tariff rate on the ith commodity, P_i and C_i are the quantities of goods produced and consumed under free-trade conditions, and ε_i and η_i are the compensated (η_i at the free-trade level of utility) own-price elasticity of supply and demand for the ith good.[14] The result (2.3) is derived by neglecting cross-price effects in production and consumption, input-output interrelationships, by assuming that some of each (private) good is produced under free trade and imported after the imposition of tariffs, and finally by ignoring terms of trade effects.

Similarly, the marginal cost of direct and indirect subsidies is equal to

$$k_s = \sum_i s_iQ_i\eta_i \qquad (2.4)$$

where s_i is the proportional rate of direct or indirect subsidization, Q_i quantity demanded of the (private) goods in the

14. See H. G. Johnson, "The Cost of Protection and the Scientific Tariff," *Journal of Political Economy* (August 1960), pp. 327–45.

absence of subsidies, and η_i the compensated (at the pre-subsidy level of utility) own-price elasticity of demand.[15] This formula derives from the assumption of constant marginal cost of production for Q_i.

If nationalization is resorted to, the marginal cost of that policy instrument is

$$k_n = \sum_i r_i\left(1 + \frac{1}{\sigma_i}\right) \tag{2.5}$$

where r_i is the rate of interest payable on the ith class of securities and σ_i is the elasticity of the marginal borrowing cost curve at the prenationalization price of securities.

Finally, the use of legislation may entail a cost which is measured by one of the formulae above or by some variation on them or it may entail a cost which is borne by the citizens of the community and therefore has no counterpart in the accounting budget of the government. If a country, for example, passed a law prohibiting the emigration of domestic brains to foreign countries, the cost of this legislation would certainly be positive but would not appear in the accounts of the government.

It can be shown that if the government is pursuing an objective of autarky, for example, and is trying to decide on whether to use outright subsidies or tariffs to achieve that goal, tariffs are less costly and consequently a better choice.[16] The effect

---

15. A. C. Harberger, "Taxation, Resource Allocation and Welfare," in *N.B.E.R. The Role of Direct and Indirect Taxes in the Federal Revenue Systems* (Princeton: Princeton University Press, 1964), pp. 25–80.

16. J. Bhagwati and V. K. Ramaswami, "Domestic Distortions, Tariffs and the Theory of Optimum Subsidies," *Journal of Political Economy* (February 1963), pp. 44–50; see also H. G. Johnson, "Tariffs and Economic Development: Some Theoretical Issues," *The Journal of Development Studies* (October 1964), pp. 3–30; If the objective was increased industrial production instead of autarky, the more efficient instrument, on the assumption of a given division of policies between objectives

of such a choice on governmental budgets should be noted. Had the government for one reason or another chosen to give subsidies to production, this would have entered the accounting budget on the expenditure side, while the selection of tariffs would mean an entry on the revenue side. The accounting effects of the choice are dramatic indeed, which is not to deny that the impact on the economic budget would be different—as we know it would—if subsidies instead of a tariff structure were chosen.

6. Institutional Arrangements

Much of the debate surrounding the definition of public (and non-private) goods has been concerned with whether these goods in fact exist. In this section I will try to show that the foregoing analysis can shed light on this problem; at the same time an important class of government policies will be described.

It will simplify matters to begin by recalling Samuelson's definition of a public good. It is a good "which all enjoy in common in the sense that each individual's consumption of such a good leads to no subtraction from any other individual's consumption of that good."[17] I suggest that for positive analysis this definition be altered to read "a public good is one which all *can* enjoy in common. . . " emphasizing thereby that even if it is technologically feasible for a good to be equally available to all, that may not be the preferred institutional arrangement, the obvious implication being that by the manipulation of policy instruments it is possible to devise institutional arrangements which restrict the availability of a public good to a smaller number of people than would be technologically possible,

---

and instruments such that tariffs and subsidies are not objectives, would be subsidies to domestic industrial production.

17. "The Pure Theory of Public Expenditures," p. 387.

even though the cost of using these instruments is not zero. In other words, we should distinguish between technological and institutional publicness.

What are the policy instruments which can be used to restrict or, more precisely, to institutionalize the availability of a good that is technologically public? They will obviously vary from good to good, but it is possible to give a number of examples. Without limiting myself to pure public goods, let me mention scramblers to forestall the reception of radio and television programs, barriers to shut off entry to an exhibition or a circus, tollgates on turnpikes to stop the free flow of circulation on a road, tickets to contemplate Caravaggio's paintings. These instruments, it should be noted, make the levy of a (necessarily non-optimal) price or user charge for the provision of a particular good and service possible; they also reflect a decision about institutional arrangements for the supply of public and non-private goods.

In addition to the implementation of the above instruments, governments can legislate on institutional arrangements. At one extreme they can decide that certain goods such as schools, parks, police protection can only be provided by the state; or along the same lines they can, by having recourse to censorship, ban certain books or films, certain religions, the use of marijuana, and a host of other goods. At the other extreme, provision of certain public goods may be left to private individuals once they have obtained a licence or a permit from the state.

It should be stressed that if a good is technologically public, it is never possible by altering the institutional form through which it is provided to transform that public good into a private one. This can be illustrated by reference to the use of unscramblers in the provision of radio and television signals.[18]

18.   On this specific case, see J. R. Minasian, "Television Pricing and

In the discussion of this problem, one might have had the impression that some contributors to the debate believed that by using unscramblers, instead of either free or commercial (i.e., based on advertising) TV, one could transform TV signals from a public into a private good. Unscramblers cannot remove the joint consumption aspect of TV; indeed, with subscription TV it would be wise for an individual who was interested in a given program and who knew that his neighbor was operating the unscrambler and watching that program on a given evening to visit him then. He would thus have free access to the TV program. One could of course argue that the two neighbors would engage in some form of bargaining à la Coase and thus internalize the public aspect of TV, but it is also possible to argue, again following Coase, that what happens in practice is that the parties find transaction costs too high and thus prefer free or commercial TV to the use of unscramblers.[19] If transaction costs were not too high and collective consumption of TV got organized in a given neighborhood, the joint consumption aspects of TV would remain even, though at the margin externalities were internalized.

Decisions about institutional arrangements always have to be made. Having determined the policy objective, the selection of policy instruments—which will determine the institutional form—will be made on efficiency grounds following the principles described in earlier sections. Therefore, if someone asserts that a technological public good should be supplied free

---

the Theory of Public Goods," *Journal of Law and Economics* (October 1964) pp. 71–80; P. A. Samuelson, "Public Goods and Subscription T.V.: Correction of the Record," *Journal of Law and Economics* (October, 1964) pp. 81–84; O. A. Davis and A. B. Whinston, "On the Distinction between Public and Private Goods," *American Economic Review* (May 1967) pp. 360–73.

19. Coase, "The Problem of Social Cost."

of direct charge, for example, he is implictly making an assumption about the proper division of policies between objectives and instruments and about the proper mix of instruments to use in the pursuit of a particular objective. Such an assertion may or may not be the one arrived at by the governing party since institutional arrangements are not in practice derived from the degree of publicness of goods or from the degree of externality they possess.

7. Competitiveness, Complementarity, and Independence

Having illustrated how one should define government output, it is important to remember that, though discussed one by one, these policies will not usually be independent of one another: some will be competitive and others complementary with each other. For example, more police protection may, by reducing the number of arsonists, imply a diminished need for fire protection. Similarly, better building or land-use standards may reduce fire hazards and thus also diminish the need for fire protection.

The relations between policies can be defined in a straight forward fashion. If, when the price (or tax-price) of public policy S_k falls, the compensated demand for S_m increases, S_k and S_m are complements; if the compensated demand for S_m falls, the two policies are substitutes; and if no change is observed in the compensated demand for S_m, we would say that the two policies are independent from the citizens' point of view.

8. Taxation

The framework used above can also serve to analyze taxation problems; again, therefore, we must distinguish between objectives and instruments. If the objective is the classical one of collecting a certain amount of revenue by introducing in the private economy the smallest number of distortions, the various instruments available to governments, such as tax bases, tax rates, exemptions, allowances, credits, loopholes, rebates, will be set at a level that will minimize welfare costs. If another objective is introduced, such as equity for a stable economy, the selection of policy instruments and the level of their operation will be different, but the principles involved in finding an efficient mix will be the same.

The situation becomes a little more complicated when we recognize that citizens will usually have no other objectives than paying the smallest possible amount of tax for any bundle of public-expenditure policies and as a consequence will have definite preferences for tax policies themselves. That is to say, citizens will have preferences among tax bases, systems of deductions, allowances, and credits because they can adjust more easily to some of these than to others. In such circumstances the policy objective of the governing party may simply be the minimization of the private (as distinguished from social) tax burdens imposed on the fraction of the electorate that is relevant for the maximization of the governing party's utility function, which, it may be recalled, is defined for a probability of reelection variable as well as for other variables to be defined in later chapters.

3

The Institutional Framework

1. Introduction

The discussion in the following chapters should make clear that the behavior of those who participate in the processes that ultimately determine the allocation of resources in the public sector—citizens, politicians, and bureaucrats—is to a large extent conditioned and influenced by the context in which these processes take place, a context that I call the institutional framework. It is therefore imperative to examine, though briefly, some of the dominant characteristics of that framework. I focus on three of them. The first, but not necessarily the most important, is the set of decision-rules that is in force at any time in a democratic society, rules known as simple majority, qualified majority, plurality, proportionality, unanimity; the second pertains to the length of the election period, defined as the number of months or of years between an election day and the next one; and the third relates to the degree of full-line supply that exists or the variety of policies on which a citizen automatically makes a choice by the simple act of voting for one representative or for one party, a phenomenon that, given the size of the public sector, is a function of whether a given society is organized as a unitary basis or as a federation and also of the extent of the existence of direct democracy.[1]

These three characteristics of the institutional framework share at least one thing: they all have the effect of shielding politicians and political parties from the preferences and the pressures of citizens. The shield is not a perfect one, of course, and the extent of its efficiency depends on the level at which the various characteristics are fixed, but unless unanimity prevails, the length of the election period is zero, and preferences count for each and every public policy separately, politicians and political parties have a number of degrees of freedom at their disposal which they can use as they please.[2] The point is of such importance and so basic to an understanding of the working of the public sector that it may be useful to restate it in a different way. Elected representatives can only retain the support of citizens if they supply the public policies desired by the latter. Each characteristic of the institutional framework separately and in combination makes it possible for politicians (and political parties) to neglect, for a time at least, the preferences of some citizens at no cost to themselves, that is without thereby necessarily jeopardizing their own position as politicians. This property of the institutional framework in turn affects the way citizens behave vis-à-vis politicians and political parties. All this should be intuitively obvious, but because of its importance and because it is usually forgotten, the present chapter will be devoted to analyzing each of the characteristics mentioned above and in subsequent chapters the characteristic which is

---

1. For another feature of the institutional framework that could conceivably have been discussed here, see chapter 8, section 6. I am referring to the constitutional rules which make it difficult (i.e., costly) for a majority to exploit the minority. Since such rules only indirectly condition how the system operates, I have not included them in this chapter.

2. I will discuss how they can be used in part 4.

relevant to an understanding of the specific behavior then under discussion will be analyzed.

2.   The Rules of Representaion

The decision-rules whereby representatives and governments are selected are in practice so numerous and so varied that it would be hopeless to try to describe and analyze every one of them; as a consequence in this section I initially focus on a simple majority, winner-take-all rule and investigate the impact of that rule on the representation of citizens' preferences; later I briefly discuss proportional representation rules. Throughout I assume that citizens have preferences for public policies and *not* for politicians, deputies, or representatives, and that these citizens can only acquire or provide themselves with these policies via a representative who, in interaction with the other representatives, must be induced and convinced to supply the policies.

In a parliamentary system of the British type, a simple majority rule operating both at the constituency level to select representatives and at the government level to select the party that will govern implies that the preferences of approximately only one-quarter of the electorate need be represented in the public sector. To see this, assume that all electoral districts are of equal size and that in each district only two candidates from only two contending parties—one of which will form the government (the cabinet or the executive)—are running for office; in each constituency the successful candidate needs only $(N + 1)/2$ votes if the number of citizens (N) is odd and $(N/2) + 1$ if it is even, while the successful party needs only $(R + 1)/2$ constituencies to form the government if the number of constituencies (R) is odd and $(R/2) + 1$ if it is even. Control of the apparatus of state can *at the limit* be effected with

$$\frac{(R + 1 + \delta_r)(N + 1 + \delta_n)}{4NR} \tag{3.1}$$

percent of the votes, where δ is zero for odd numbers and one for even numbers of voters and of constituencies. As R and/or N increase without bound, (3.1) goes to 0.25.

It must be emphasized that 25 percent is a limit. It is so in the obvious sense that N and/or R must increase without bound for it to obtain, but also in the sense that a party will be reelected by meeting the preferences of 25 percent of the electorate, only if that 25 percent is distributed over constituencies in a very special way. In practice, some votes will be wasted in that in many constituencies successful candidates will obtain more than the share of the votes that is strictly required to be elected. As a result, a higher percentage of votes will be obtained, but it remains true that a party could remain in office with the support of only 25 percent of the electorate provided that this support is optimally distributed.

If electoral districts are of unequal size but the number of contending candidates and parties is still limited to two the percentage of the electorate that needs to be represented in the public sector for the governing party to remain in office may fall below 25 percent, since a party could—and, assuming that the cost of gaining votes is positive, that parties seek reelection at the lowest possible cost, and that uncertainty is absent, would —disregard the preferences of citizens in larger constituencies and focus on majorities in a sufficiently large number of the smaller districts to remain in office. This is the immediate consequence of the fact that each constituency is represented by only one man and partly explains the great importance of rural electoral districts in a number of countries where farmers are only a very small proportion of the electorate. It is, however, not as easy in this case to define the exact proportion of citizens whose preferences must be satisfied if the governing party is going to regain office since this proportion will vary with the distribution of constituencies by size. It is, however, possible to say that at the limit that number will never be larger than 0.25, and will in general be smaller than that.

If the number of competing political parties or candidates is increased, but the size of electoral districts—measured by the number of citizens—is again assumed to be equal, we have a situation that resembles that examined in the previous paragraph since it is again possible for a party to be returned to power with less than 25 percent of the vote—again disregarding wasted votes. This time the exact proportion depends on the relative electoral strength of the contending parties and it is difficult to define it exactly. However, if we assume that the parties are of approximately equal strength, a politician needs a number of votes equal to only $[(N + a)/3] + 1$ to be elected (a is a number which takes the value of 0, 1, or 2 depending on the value of N), and if $(R/2) + 1$ (R even) constituencies are needed to form the government, *at the limit* only 16.6 percent of the voters need to be represented if the governing party is to retain power. However, if the parties are of unequal strength, as is usually the case, the percentage of the electorate that must be represented will be larger than 16.6 percent, but will not exceed 25 percent.

In contrast to the decision-rules in the parliamentary system, the rules governing the choice of the president and of the governors of each state in the American congressional system require the support of a larger fraction of the electorate. Indeed, if the number of voting citizens N is odd, at least $(N + 1)/2$ favorable votes are required for election if only two candidates are running for office. As a proportion of the electorate that number goes to 0.50 as N goes to infinity. One should not infer from this that a congressional system is more representative than a parliamentary system since the presidency is only a part—albeit an important part—of the congressional system. Not much can be said without a detailed consideration of the role of congress. The above discussion was meant to illustrate the working and the importance of decision-rules as well as the variations that exist within the class of rules known as simple majority, winner-take-all rules.

These rules are far from being the only existing ones governing the choice of representatives and/or governments. In practice one also finds a large number of rules of proportional representation whereby the number of elected representatives tends to be roughly divided in proportion to the number of votes a party receives. One cannot deny that proportional representation increases the minimum size of the group of citizens whose preferences a governing party must satisfy in principle to 50 percent.[3] However, the problem of nonrepresentation is often transferred to a second higher level, namely, to the level of the formation of the government. In other words, with proportional representation, it will often, though not always, be necessary to resort to the formation of a coalition government. When this happens, members of all parties may not be included in the coalition since the elected members of two or three parties may constitute a large enough number of representatives to produce the winning coalition. But even if all parties were represented in the coalition, decisions could only be made by using some non-unanimity decision-rule, that is, by sacrificing the preferences of some citizens.[4]

Let me end by adding that it is tempting to argue that un-

---

3. For a discussion of proportional representation, see G. Tullock, *Toward a Mathematics of Politics* (Ann Arbor: University of Michigan Press, 1967), chapter 10.

4. This point has been developed at length by Downs; see *An Economic Theory of Democracy*, chapter 9.

animity is the only rule that insures that the preferences of all citizens count in the decision-making process, but unanimity is not a rule that accords easily with representative democracy, though it has some appeal for direct democracy. Indeed that rule is totally impracticable without the existence of implicit or explicit side payments which insure that votes can be bought off (presumably at an equilibrium price, though the certainty of this never exists) and that a decision is reached. Side payments are tolerably easy to visualize when they involve goods and services, but they are more difficult to imagine when the object of the bargain are representatives since these necessarily represent citizens for a large number of policies and side payments are not as easily attached to specific policies. If representatives had to supply only one policy, side payments would be easier to imagine, but then this would not be representative democracy, but a disguised form of direct democracy.

If unanimity is not really a practicable decision-rule and if all the other rules lead, to a greater or to a lesser extent, to the neglect of the preferences of some citizens, a knowledge and an understanding of the working of the public sector and of the level and composition of public expenditure and taxation will require that we know which preferences count and which ones do not in the process of decision-making and resource allocation. That is the task before us.

3.   The Election Period

In many ways the length of the election period may be the most important of the three characteristics of the institutional framework that I have chosen to emphasize, even though it has received very little attention in the literature. Its importance comes from the fact that, given that a political party has a number of years before it has to run for reelection, there is scarcely anything that can be done during that period to influence it *if it decides that it is not going to be influenced.* There is indeed much that can be explained in the behavior of politicians and political parties by simply considering the number of years before the next election. Grand designs, far-reaching plans, and long perspectives are usually the prerogative of those politicians who can visualize themselves in office for some years, and if we take dictatorships to be democracies with an election period of infinite length (an assumption that is not really legitimate), that prerogative is especially theirs.

In later chapters I will explain how this feature of the institutional framework influences the working of various hypotheses related to the behavior of citizens and politicians, but in this chapter I wish to emphasize that an election period of non-zero length automatically provides politicians and political parties with some freedom to implement policies which may be at variance with the preferences of some or even all citizens and this at no cost to themselves—at least for a period of time. There is no doubt, therefore, that a model which is aimed at explaining the behavior of public expenditures and taxation, not only for the years approaching election years but on a continuous basis, must take this characteristic of the election system into account.

From the point of view of citizens, an election period of positive, but finite, length implies that the cost of influencing politicians by voting is infinite during all of that period. As I will argue in chapter 6, this is one of the reasons why citizens engage in other political activities—lobbies, pressure groups, social movements, private provision, political mobility— besides voting and accounts for the fact that voting is far from being the only influential (or even the most important) factor in the determination of the composition and level of public output.

4. A Full-Line Supply

An essential trait of representative democracies (in fact, their raison d'être) is that elected representatives have the task of providing citizens not with one policy but with a *bundle* of public policies. Though often advertised as radical changes, these policies are usually either marginal changes in existing policies or new marginal policies, but in any case they are bundles of policies or bundles of changes in policies. This implies that a vote for a representative is a vote for a full bundle of policies. As a result of this aspect of the institutional framework—which I have called full-line supply in analogy with the full-line forcing sometimes practiced by large conglomerates—politicians have the freedom to supply a number of public policies which are at variance with some of the preferences even of those citizens who support them.

To see this, one needs reflect on the fact that a citizen will choose the candidate who promises to supply those policies on which he places a high value, even if by so doing he also has to accept policies which he positively dislikes. To put it differently, a citizen will choose among candidates the one who offers the bundle of policies with the highest expected utility even though this may imply accepting policies he does not like. If there are only two candidates, C and D, each offering a bundle of policies S_1, S_2, . . . S_n (some of which may be zero), the expected utility derived by one citizen from C's offer is

$$E(U_C) = U(S_{1C}, S_{2C}, . . ., S_{nC}) \qquad (3.2)$$

and that derived by the same citizen from the offer of candidate D is

$$E(U_D) = U(S_{1D}, S_{2D}, . . ., S_{nD}) \qquad (3.3)$$

where the S's are amounts of public policies. It should be clear that $E(U_C)$ can be greater that $E(U_D)$ even if some $S_C < S_D$.

It follows from this that candidate C (or D) need not adjust all the S's to the preference level of a given citizen to obtain his support.

It is of some interest to note in concluding that federalism and direct democracy both have the effect of reducing the size of the bundle of policies over which a candidate and a party have control and thus at the same time reducing their freedom to trade policies one against the other without regard to the preferences of citizens. Federalism and direct democracy thus reduce the extent of full-line supply and as such strengthen the link between the performance of politicians and the preferences of citizens.[5]

5. A Normative Note on Democracy

In the preceding discussion, I have not analyzed the factors that determined the decision-rules in force, the length of the election period, and the extent of full-line supply because I take these characteristics of the institutional framework to be exogenous data in the analysis of government expenditure and taxation. Such an analysis based on the costs and advantages of alternative levels of these characteristics could, however, provide us with a theory of the structure of democracy.

Indeed, by defining the costs and the benefits of alternative levels of these characteristics, one could determine the optimum degree of democracy achievable at any given time. Much of the normative literature on democracy and all welfare economics are really utopian since they assume that democracy can only exist if the decision-rule is unanimity, if the length of the elec-

5. Much of what is relevant to this question can be found in J. R. Pennock, "Federal and Unitary Government—Disharmony and Frustration," *Behavioral Science* (April 1959) pp. 147–57. See also below chapter 6, section 5.

tion period is zero, and if full-line supply has been eliminated. Between utopia and the optimum there may, however, be quite a large gap; it is not the task of this study to examine this most interesting and pressing issue.[6]

6. Conclusion

In concluding this chapter, I wish to point out that even if I have discussed the characteristics of the institutional framework separately, in practice they are related to each other. As a consequence until we have measured the number of degrees of freedom that each characteristic gives to politicians to pursue private objectives unrelated to the preferences of citizens and until we know the strength of the incentive that these same characteristics give to citizens to participate in the political process by engaging in activities other than voting, we are not in a position to compare political systems. Empirical research should, however, eventually tell us the rate of substitution that exists between decision-rules, length of election periods, and full-line supply as these influence the freedom of politicians and the incentive of citizens. It will not, however, be possible to make these empirical discoveries until we know what questions to ask, that is, until we have developed a more complete theoretical model. To this task I now turn.

6. Much of what is relevant to such a discussion can be found in Buchanan and Tullock, *The Calculus of Consent*.

II

The Structure of Demand

quote

The possibility, therefore, of high costs in the exchange relationship
is quite great in the sense that something is lost in the transfer.
This is seen particularly in the political relationship, in which the
terms of trade of the individual with the state are often very bad
indeed. The individual gives up a great deal in terms of being
taxed, conscripted, killed or injured in wars, and burdened with
the guilt of murder and destruction; in return the state seems to
give him little, except perhaps a bit of security and a larger identity.
It is not surprising, therefore, that we have been urged to ask not
what our country can do for us but what we can do for our country.
The first question might prove to be too embarrassing.

K. E. BOULDING

4

The Origins of Political Action

1. Introduction

It is usual in economic theory to assume that consumers engage in only one type of economic activity: the purchase or sale of goods and services. The other activities in which they engage —window-shopping, swapping of recipes and advice, experimenting with new products, acquiring information on goods and services and on their prices and suppliers—are not considered to be significant aspects of behavior for the specific purpose of studying the market mechanism through which some scarce resources are allocated. The origin of the postualted action is simple: a consumer with given preferences and a given income faces a set of goods and services each of which can be traded at a given price; for each of these goods, the consumer can, taking his tastes, his income, and the prices of goods as fixed, determine the quantities he desires. If he has less than these quantities, he buys; if he has more, he sells.

Since changes in his preferences, in his income, and/or in the prices of commodities will change the quantities a consumer will desire, they will lead to changes in the amounts bought or

55

sold. To predict whether the quantities bought or sold are larger or smaller than before the change in tastes, income, or prices, one must impose some restrictions on the preferences of consumers, restrictions which are all basically empirical in nature.

In analyzing the behavior of citizens, we will not be able to restrict to one the number of activities in which they engage simply because citizens cannot individually buy or sell public policies if the amounts supplied to them are different from the amounts desired, and hence because adjustments in their budgets cannot be achieved directly. But we will assume that the quantities of public policies that are desired are determined by the same kind of forces that determine the amount of goods and services desired by consumers: the own-price of the policy, the price of other policies, goods and services, income, and preferences for public policies as well as for private goods and services. This chapter will be principally concerned with these forces and therefore with the determination of the desired amounts of public policies. But since citizens cannot directly and individually adjust the quantities of public policies they are supplied with to the amount that they desire—a phenomenon that depends on the public and non-private goods characteristics of many of these policies—the difference between the two magnitudes plays a more central role when decisions are collective or public than when they are private and as a consequence more space will be devoted to it.[1]

In the remainder of this study, I will call the difference (whether positive or negative) between the amount desired of public policies (at existing tax-prices and incomes) and that provided,

1. Since the essential properties of public goods are found in non-private goods, the argument of this chapter (and, indeed, of this study) is developed solely for the former, but is applicable to both types of goods. See Appendix I, where it is shown that the basic characteristics of pure public goods extend to non-private goods.

the degree of coercion imposed on citizens, and I will assume that coercion is (absolutely) greater, the larger the difference between the two magnitudes. This is not a completely happy choice of words, but it emphasizes the difference between the situation of a consumer who is in a state of disequilibrium but capable of engaging directly in actions that will remove the disequilibrium, and that of a citizen who is also in a state of disequilibrium but unable to buy or to sell and therefore only able to affect his own position by influencing politicians.

I must immediately point out that nowhere do I assume that governments coerce citizens because they derive satisfaction from that act or because they want to do so; instead coercion originates as the by-product of a fundamental property of public goods. Because pure public goods are, by definition, made equally available to every citizen in a jurisdiction, consumption is necessarily collective; this, in turn, implies one or the other of two things. If the distribution over citizens of the total cost of supplying a public good is given, any change in the quantity provided must be one that improves the situation of some individuals while worsening that of others unless the amount provided is so small relative to what is desired by *all* citizens that everyone wants more or vice versa (for supplies that are large relative to what is desired by all). Alternatively, if the quantity supplied is given, each citizen will discover that the amount he has to pay for the policy depends upon the amount paid by others. The second of these propositions is the obverse of the first. Both imply that voluntary or coercion-free organization to supply public policies is basically impossible for the large group, though in smaller groups cooperation between individuals may lead to a coercion-free situation.

The nature of the problem can be stated as follows: initially the governing party must make decisions about the pattern and quantity of public policy (both expenditure and tax policies) without any knowledge about the preferences of citizens.[2] The initial decisions of governing parties must therefore always be somewhat arbitrary and hence must place some citizens in a state of coercion. Such a situation, however, cannot be a final one, since it will set in motion forces that will operate to reduce or, possibly for some citizens, to eliminate the initial coercion that has been imposed on them.

This chapter does not examine the ways and means through which coercion can be reduced—that is the task of the next chapter—but examines the nature of coercion in three different models of individual adjustment to government action. Two of these models—one in which only one public good is assumed to exist and a second in which more than one such good is postulated—are strictly valid only for small departures from any given configuration of tax and expenditure policies. The third model is an aggregate model that is valid for other than marginal changes.

There are two ways of justifying the marginalist model for positive empirical analysis: one can first assume that the tax-prices paid by citizens do not vary as the quantity of the public goods supplied varies and therefore that marginal and average tax-prices are equal,[3] or, second, one can assume that changes in government tax and expenditure policies are always marginal changes.[4] A justification for the first assumption would simply be that in fact changes in government policies are marginal ones and that, therefore, in practice marginal tax-prices *appear*

2. The theory developed in this book is not dynamic (but only comparative statical) and therefore propositions such as "in the first instance," "initially," or "in the initial situation," when they do not apply to equilibrium situations, only have heuristic value.

3. This is the assumption adopted by Buchanan in *The Demand and Supply of Public Goods;* see his discussion of the problem in chapter 3.

4. This is Downs' assumption in *An Economic Theory of Democracy,* p. 52 and following.

to all to be constant. However, to dispose of the problem of the indeterminacy of the distribution of the infra-marginal surplus over citizens, constancy of marginal tax-prices over all amounts of public policies must be assumed. Note that a model that is valid only "in the small" may be sufficient for a theory of coercion that provides motivation for political participation unless changes in public expenditure and tax policies are generally achieved *without* altering the marginal valuation of public policies by any citizen—a theoretical possibility but not an empirically very likely one. In any case because of this possibility, I suggest an alternative model in section 4 below.

2.   A World with Only One Public Good

Our first task in developing the basic marginalist model is to define the optimal or desired situation for each citizen taken in isolation; the second task is to compare that desired position with the actual or existing one. There are two alternative, but equivalent, ways of defining the desired situation. One can, for example, impute to each citizen (j) well-behaved, concave, ordinal utility functions defined for private (x) and public (S) goods and assume that these are maximized subject to budget constraints defined in terms of *given* prices for private goods and *given* tax-prices for public goods. The alternative approach recognizes *even at the level of individual adjustment* that public goods, in whatever quantities they are supplied, are made available equally to every citizen and as a consequence utility functions are defined for private goods and tax-prices and maximized subject to budget constraints formulated in terms of given prices for private goods, but given quantities of public goods.

If we restrict ourselves to one private and one public good, the first approach can be summarized as follows: to maximize

$$U^j = U^j (X, S) \qquad (j = 1, \ldots, J) \qquad (4.1)$$

subject to

$$I^j = \bar{p}_x X + \bar{q}^j S \qquad (j = 1, \ldots, J) \qquad (4.2)$$

where p_x is the market price of X, q^j are the tax-prices of S—assumed to differ from citizen to citizen (hence the superscript ^{j})—and the bars over the prices indicate that they are exogenously given.[5]

The second alternative starts from the definition of public goods itself, namely that

$$\bar{S} = S^1 = S^2 = \ldots = S^J \qquad (4.3)$$

and therefore formulates the problem as that of maximizing

$$U^j = U^j(X, q) \qquad (j = 1, \ldots, J) \qquad (4.4)$$

subject to

$$I^j = \bar{p}_x X + q\bar{S}. \qquad (j = 1, \ldots, J) \qquad (4.5)$$

The maximum in the first case is given by

$$U_x{}^j(X, S) = \frac{\partial U^j}{\partial X} = \lambda \bar{P}_x$$
$$\qquad (j = 1, \ldots, J) \qquad (4.6)$$
$$U_s{}^j(X, S) = \frac{\partial U^j}{\partial S} = \lambda \bar{q}^j$$

where $\lambda(\neq 0)$ is an undetermined lagrangean multiplier, measuring the marginal utility of money income. Assuming that X is the numéraire and setting $p_x = 1$, (4.6) reduces to

$$\frac{U_s{}^j}{U_x{}^j} = \bar{q}^j \qquad (j = 1, \ldots, J) \qquad (4.7)$$

5. Instead of "tax-prices," one could use the expression "pseudo-prices" as Samuelson has done in a recent paper. See P. A. Samuelson, "The Pure Theory of Public Expenditure and Taxation," in *Public Economics*.

which tells us that the desired quantity of S by citizen j is the amount that makes the marginal rate of substitution between S and the numéraire equal to the tax-prices of S.

The second problem's maximum turns out to be

$$\frac{\partial U^j}{\partial X} - \lambda \bar{p}_x = 0$$

$$\frac{\partial U^j}{\partial q} - \lambda \bar{S} = 0 \qquad (j = 1, \ldots, J) \qquad (4.8)$$

which again, assuming X to be the numéraire and $P_x = 1$, reduces to

$$\frac{U_q^j}{U_x^j} = \bar{S} \qquad (j = 1, \ldots, J) \qquad (4.9)$$

an expression which tells us that the desired tax-price for $\bar{S}$ of S is the one which equates the marginal utility of foregone private good to the marginal utility of the private good itself.[6]

By solving (4.7) together with (4.2) or (4.9) with (4.5), we can derive the following implicit expression

$$F^j(S^j, q^j, I^j) = 0 \qquad (j = 1, \ldots, J) \qquad (4.10)$$

which can be given the explicit form

$$S^j = F^j(q^j, I^j) \qquad (j = 1, \ldots, J) \qquad (4.11)$$

We need a name for these relationships. In the remainder of this chapter, I will call them "technocratic demand functions" to emphasize the fact that they are demand curves derived from basic data-utility functions and budget constraints—but that, as they stand, they have no institutional existence. Since citizens cannot individually buy or sell public goods, technocratic demand functions as defined by (4.11) are not revealed in the public sector; they only tell us that given some value of q^j and

---

6. It may be easier to visualize this by rewriting (4.9) as $U_x^j = \dfrac{q^j}{S}$

I^j, let us say q^{*j} and I^{*j}, the amount of S that citizen j will *desire* is S^{*j}—a quantity that can easily be different from the one supplied by the governing party.

The fact that a pure public good must be made available equally to all citizens—that (4.3) must hold—does not alter the basic nature of (4.10) and (4.11). Indeed, we can always insure that any quantity of S—let us say S^0—will be the desired quantity for every citizen by choosing values of q^j that will make S^0 the desired amount, for given sizes of I^j. Let us call these values of q^j, q^{0j}. Since the technocratic demand functions F^j (q^j, I^j) vary between citizens, the q^{0j} will also vary if (4.7) is to hold. In other words, tax-prices will be different for different citizens if these latter are going to be on their technocratic demand functions.

Note also that differentiating (4.11) with respect to q^j will produce the usual Slutsky equation, dividing a price change into substitution and income effects. Indeed, that differentiation will yield

$$\frac{dS^j}{dq^j} = \frac{\partial S^j}{\partial q^j} + \frac{\partial S^j}{\partial I^j}\frac{\partial I^j}{\partial q^j} \tag{4.12}$$

an expression which can be manipulated to produce

$$\frac{\partial S^j}{\partial q^j} = \frac{\partial S^j}{\partial q^j} + S^j\frac{\partial S^j}{\partial I^j} \tag{4.13}$$

As a statement of desire or of optimality for the individual citizen taken in isolation, technocratic demand functions do not differ from other standard demand functions. The difference arises out of the fact that citizens cannot individually buy or sell public goods.

In a world in which only one public good exists and in which debt-financing in all forms is ruled out, it is necessary to assume that the sum of the tax-prices paid by all citizens is equal to the marginal cost of supplying a given amount of S and consequently we have

$$\sum_{j=1}^{J} q^{j*} = c^* \tag{4.14}$$

where c^* is the marginal cost (measured in terms of X) of S^* of S and the q^{*j}'s are the desired tax-prices. Since

$$q^{j*} = \frac{U_{s*}^{j}}{U_{x}^{j}} \tag{4.15}$$

we must also have

$$\sum_{j} q^{j*} = \sum_{j} \frac{U_{s*}^{j}}{U_{x}^{j}} = c^* \tag{4.16}$$

which states that the sum over citizens of the marginal rates of substitution of S for X is equal to the sum of the desired tax-prices paid by citizens and that these two magnitudes in turn are equal to the marginal private good cost of S, that is, to the marginal rate of transformation of S for X. Observe that (4.16) will hold only if the q^j's are so chosen that (4.9), the first-order conditions for a maximum of (4.4), hold. If $q^j \neq U_s^j/U_x^j$, an important part of (4.16) will not hold, even though we still can insure that the $\sum_{j} q^j = c$.

Indeed, it is with this inequality, which is pervasive throughout the public sector, that coercion makes its appearance. That the inequality will often exist can easily be seen by recognizing that citizens cannot in a system of representative democracy select either the amount of S they desire or the level of q that would maximize their welfare. In the economics of private goods, when an inequality of this type arises, it is assumed that the consumer will individually buy or sell private goods to reestablish the equality of the marginal rate of substitution with the ruling price. Since citizens cannot individually buy or sell public goods, we will have to investigate in some detail the impact of the inequality on their behavior. Suffice it to say at this point that an inequality between $U_s{}^j/U_x{}^j$ and q^j will lead to political participation although, as we shall see later on, this is only a sufficient condition for political participation. Indeed, I assume that the greater the difference between the two magnitudes, the larger the degree of coercion and hence the larger the extent of political participation.

Part of the foregoing argument may be clarified by the use of two simple diagrams. Assume two citizens A and B portrayed by two compensated demand curves also called A and B in figure 4.1; assume a positively sloped marginal cost curve labeled c which, given the sum of the tax-prices charged to A and B, tells us what will be the amount of public good supplied or, alternatively, given the amount of S provided, tells us the amount of revenue that is needed to cover the costs of supply. We can develop the argument by assuming either that S is given or that the tax-prices q_a and q_b are given. Let us make the first assumption and assume that S^* of S is provided. If the tax-price charged to or levied on A is equal to $q_a{}^*$ and that on B is $q_b{}^*$ in such a way that $q_a{}^* + q_b{}^* = q$ and if $q_a{}^*$ and $q_b{}^*$ are each equal to A and B's respective marginal rate of substitution of S for X, then desired and actual magnitudes of all variables are equal and the degree of coercion imposed on A and B is zero. If, however, S^* of S is still the amount of the public good supplied, but $q_a{}^0$ is the tax-price charged to A and $q_b{}^0$ that charged to B, again insuring that $q_a{}^0 + q_b{}^0 = q$, but not that they be equal respectively to A and to B's marginal rate of substitution, we will have an absolute positive degree of coercion.

To see this it is sufficient to note that when $q_a{}^0$ is the tax-price levied on him, A will desire S_a of S while S^* is supplied; similarly, with a tax-price of $q_b{}^0$, B wants S_b and receives S^*. The degree of coercion imposed on A when $q_a{}^0$ charged is equal to

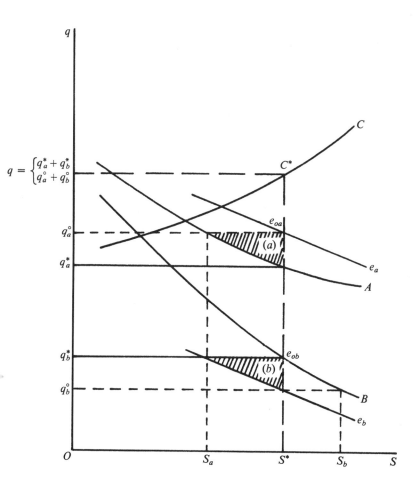

$$q = \begin{cases} q_a^* + q_b^* \\ q_a^\circ + q_b^\circ \end{cases}$$

FIGURE   4.1

the (approximate) triangle labeled (*a*), and that imposed on *B* is equal to the area (*b*). The fact that the tax-prices are set at such a level that the revenue of the government is sufficient to cover costs does not insure that coercion does not exist.

Let me emphasize the meaning that is given to the concept of coercion in this analysis by focusing exclusively on citizen *A*. Consider again figure 4. We have seen that *A* would not be coerced if q_a^* was the marginal tax-price he faced, but he is required to pay q_a^0 and as a consequence he cannot be on his technocratic demand curve, that is, on the curve describing his desired positions. Instead he will be at a point such as e_{0b} on e_b. That last curve could be called a "coercion demand curve" since it does not reflect utility maximization, but only the government's estimate of *A*'s demand. In essence, therefore, it is not a demand curve at all, since *A* cannot be expected to stay on it, though he will initially be placed on it. Before proceeding, I should point out that the shape of e_b (and of e_a) is unknown and that it cannot be derived from first principles since it only reflects guesses on the part of the government. It is a curve that is imposed on *A*. Another way of describing the phenomenon is to say that if *A* could obtain a reduction in the amount of *S* that is provided (q_a^0 remaining unchanged), he would do so since the increased purchase of the private good that this would make possible is worth more to him than the excess of S^* over S_a is.

3.   A World with Two or More Public Goods

The preceding analysis assumed that individuals had preferences for only one private good and one public good, and as a consequence that governments provided only one of the last type of policies. Surely, citizens want more than one public good and governments accordingly supply them with more than one such good. The technocratic solution to the problem is not affected by this extension, as is easily verified, but the institutional problem is much more complicated.[7] These complications all arise from the fact that the imputation of tax-prices to each public policy is much more difficult than in the one good case. Indeed, in models in which it is assumed that only one public good exists, it seems reasonable to suppose, as I did above, that the total amount of taxes paid by a citizen divided by the number of units of public policy supplied by the government is an acceptable measure of the tax-price actually paid by the citizen. However, when two or more public goods are supplied, it is not clear what is the best assumption that one can make since the proper division of the proceeds of an income tax, say, between two or more goods is not at all obvious. In fact, in all of the various ways one can imagine to deal with this problem, there is a strong element of arbitrariness involved. One could assume, for example, that each citizen has an expectation of the marginal tax base and/or marginal tax rate that would be changed if the governing party was to increase the amount supplied of policy S_1 by one unit, policy S_2 by one unit, and so on for all policies. This vector of expected marginal tax-prices could then be compared with the desired marginal tax-prices.

Other assumptions could be made. But there is no way, given our existing empirical knowledge, of denying the essential arbitrariness of any of these assumptions. In the next section, I will, in effect, assume that technocratic demand functions do not exist for each and every policy taken separately, but only for groups of policies. If this turned out to be a reasonable assumption—and only careful and systematic empirical work will reveal this—tax-shares would be the variables that would have

7. See, for example, Samuelson's "The Pure Theory of Public Expenditure."

to be related to public policy classes or groups.

The most efficient way of deriving the characteristics of the desired—that is, the coercion-free—bundle of tax and expenditure policies is to recognize, as we did in the previous section, that in competitive markets for private goods, the prices at which these goods are purchased by consumers are given, while in the case of public provision of public goods, it is the quantities of the goods themselves that are given. Consequently, in defining the equilibrium for private goods, it is the quantities of these goods that have to be adjusted to the given prices, while for public goods it is the marginal (equal to average) tax-prices that have to be adjusted to given quantities.

The reasoning can be formalized by assuming a utility function for each citizen (j) defined for flows of private goods and services (X) and for the tax-prices of public goods (q) thus:

$$U^j = U^j(X_1, \ldots, X_n; q_1, \ldots, q_m) \quad (j = 1, \ldots, J) \quad (4.17)$$

to be maximized subject to

$$I^j = \bar{p}_1 X_1{}^j + \cdots + \bar{p}_n X_n{}^j + q_i{}^j \bar{S}_1 + \cdots$$
$$+ q_m{}^j \bar{S}_m \ (j = 1, \ldots, J) \quad (4.18)$$

where the bars over the p's and the S's indicate that the level of these variables must be taken as given. It would be useless to repeat with (4.17) and (4.18) what would, in effect, be an essentially similar exercise as the one conducted in the previous section. I will therefore examine diagramatically (figure 4.2) the main effect of increasing the number of public goods from one to two, namely, the appearance of substitutes and complements.

Let me therefore focus again on citizen A—the analysis applying mutatis mutandis to all other citizens—whose utility function is defined for two public goods S_1 and S_2 and for only one private good X. The government provides S^*_1 of S_1 and

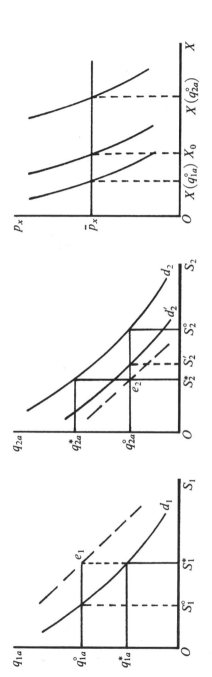

FIGURE. 4.2

S^*_2 of S_2 and levies q^0_{1a} and q^0_{2a} to pay for these goods, while A would be willing to pay q^*_{1a} and q^*_{2a} for the goods—the two last numbers being those that would remove all coercion. This is portrayed in figure 4.2, where it is also assumed, to make the problem specific, that $q^*_{1a} < q^0_{1a}$ and that $q^*_{2a} < q^0_{2a}$.

To proceed, start by focusing attention exclusively on S_2 in the center panel and note that at q^0_{2a}, A is provided with S^*_2 of S_2 which is less than S^0_2, the amount he desires at that tax-price, so that his coercion (or institutional) demand curve for S_2 passes through e_2 and his demand curve for X, initially at X_0, now slides to the right to $X(q^0_{2a})$—the quantity of X taken when $\bar{p}_x$ is the price of X. Since the value A places on a marginal unit of X is less than the value he places on a marginal unit of S_2, and since there is nothing that he can, initially at least, do about it, A is being coerced. Now assume that the government decides to provide S^*_1 of S_1 at q^0_{1a}. If we temporarily disregard any relation that could exist between S_1 and S_2, we note that the action of the government will mean that the coercion demand curve for S_1 will pass through e_1 and that the demand curve for X will slide to the left to $X(q^0_{1a})$. Suppose, however, that S_1 is a substitute for S_2. This implies that the technocratic demand curve for S_2—the one describing desired positions and labeled d in figure 4.2—will shift to the left, from d_2 to d_2', once S^*_1 is made available, so that at q^0_{2a}, the desired amount of S_2 will fall from S^0_2 to S^1_2 and thus approach S^*_2, the amount that is actually supplied. The demand for X may be larger or smaller than it is when S_1 and S_2 are independent of one another; in figure 4.2, it is assumed to be smaller. If S_1 and S_2 had been complements instead of substitutes, the technocratic demand curve for S_2 would have shifted to the right and coercion in S_2 as well as in S_1 would have been increased.

The foregoing argument is of much importance in understanding observed government behavior. Often a governing party will try to eliminate coercion generated by the provision of one public policy by altering the supply, not of that policy, but of other policies which are either substitutes or complementary to it. To illustrate, assume that the government cannot implement optimal (from the economist's point of view) fiscal and monetary policies to combat an increase in the level of unemployment because of the opposition of dominant members of the bureaucracy to these policies. In such circumstances, the only policies that the governing party can implement are substitute policies (pension programs, social security provisions, reduction in military commitments, etc.) designed to reduce the degree of coercion generated by the unemployment. Whether or not it will be successful in that endeavor is a different question and one to which I will return in later chapters.

Finally, observe that even if it is possible to sum the degree of coercion that attaches to each public policy for citizen j by summing the absolute values of triangles over all m policies, it must, however, be remembered that some coercion will lead citizens to demand more of some public expenditure policies and/or to pay lower marginal tax-prices for them, while other coercion will lead to demands for smaller expenditures, though not to demands for higher tax-prices.

4. An Aggregative Model

A model that assumes constant marginal (and average) tax-prices is useful and in practice is certainly able to carry us pretty far—though this is essentially an empirical question and no amount of conceptual debate can hope to resolve it—but, in principle, it is a restrictive one. The extension of the model to variable marginal tax-prices, however, implies that individual technocratic demand curves cease to be single-valued. Indeed, variable marginal tax-prices over changing amounts of public policies means that the infra-marginal surplus is indeterminate and as a consequence the degree of coercion is also indeterminate, except at the margin, since a new technocratic demand curve is defined for each new allocation of the infra-marginal surplus. Because of the difficulties inherent in this approach, but especially because of the paucity of empirically meaningful results of such a model, I have chosen to suggest an "aggregative" model and not to inquire at this point into the individual behavior that underlies that model.

The model rests on the assumption that citizens have some idea of what constitutes a fair burden of taxation for them, an assumption that does not imply that they would not appreciate a reduction in the amount of tax they have to pay. The idea of what is fair (and unfair) is related, I assume, to the value of the bundle of policies that the governing party makes available to them. Indeed, it seems plausible to assume that the idea of what is fair and unfair is closely related to what citizens desire or do not desire in the way of public expenditure policies. If this is the case, a calculus, akin to the one developed in the two previous sections for marginal changes in policies, would most certainly underlie the comparison between the subjective value of tax payments and the subjective value of expenditure receipts, though in this case one must assume that the calculus would involve both the marginal and the infra-marginal magnitudes.

If a tax burden—whose value is subjectively determined in relation to the value of public benefits received—is deemed unfair, a citizen will feel coerced and because of this will be motivated to participate in the political process. Alternatively, if a tax burden is seen to be fair, coercion will not exist, and as a result a citizen will not engage in political action unless he expects the activities of other citizens to be successful and to result ultimately in a situation of coercion.

Note that if citizens or groups of citizens have roughly similar tastes and if the policies supplied by the government have strong public goods characteristics, citizens could easily think of tax burdens as being tax shares since in such circumstances the marginal value of the benefits would tend to be the same for all citizens and the point of comparison would inevitably be the share of the total cost paid by each as this relates to income or other similar variables. In such a case, the model about tax burdens would apply to tax shares.

Even if the foregoing statement of the model is made in terms of tax burdens or tax shares, it would be possible and logically equivalent to say that citizens have an idea of what constitutes an acceptable level of public expenditure and that this idea is defined in relation to the amount of taxes that they have to pay. Put in this alternative form, the motivational forces inherent in the model do not differ much from those to be found in the model proposed by Peacock and Wiseman, though their model was not one about participation in the political process, but about the determination of expenditure levels.[8]

8. A. T. Peacock and J. Wiseman, *The Growth of Public Expenditure in the United Kingdom* (New Edition, London; Allen & Unwin, 1967), chapter 2. For some notes on Peacock and Wiseman's model, see Appendix 2.

5

The Instruments of Political Participation

1.   Introduction

This chapter examines the various activities in which utility-maximizing citizens can engage in an effort to reduce, or even to eliminate, the coercion (or the expected coercion) that is placed on them by the government's supply of policies with public and non-private goods characteristics.[1] The object of the chapter could also be defined as that of analyzing how individual citizens, motivated by their own interest, can seek to achieve partial or complete elimination of the coercion (or of the expected coercion) imposed on them by the governing party and in the process signal or reveal their (positive or negative) preferences for public policies. Throughout I assume that citizens deal with politicians and political parties that maximize a utility function defined, among other things, for probability of reelection variable so that it makes sense to assume that citizens can influence the pattern of government policies.

Citizens have preferences for expenditure and tax policies and thus will seek redress from a coercive situation by working

1.   See section 2 below.

for changes either in expenditure policies or in tax policies or in both. They will do this by engaging in activities—or what, given the nature of the problem, will in practice often (but not always) turn out to be support for or opposition to political parties—which will take many forms; the following discussion examines seven such activities. Listed in the order in which I shall describe and analyze them they are: (1) participating in efforts to influence the actions of lobbies and large pressure groups; (2) engaging in actions to influence politicians directly; (3) joining social movements; (4) regulating one's own private economic behavior: (5) organizing the private provision of public and non-private goods; (6) moving from one jurisdiction to another; and (7) voting or the act of giving one's support to or withholding it from a candidate of a political party or, in very special cases, a policy.

Note immediately that the first three and the last of these activities are directly aimed at influencing politicians and political parties into altering their policies, while the three others are only indirectly oriented toward that objective. These last activities—namely moving, self-provision, and the regulation of one's private economic behavior—seek the removal of coercion outside the traditional frontiers of the political arena. They are the only activities (with the exception of voting) which have historically been examined by economists who have thus implicitly assumed that these were the only possible modes of adjustment to coercive situations.

Before proceeding to the analysis of these activities, one point should be made about the place of voting in the set of all political activities. There is a very real sense in which voting is different from the other political activities through which citizens seek to remove the coercion imposed on them since voting is the activity which determines whether or not a politician and/or a political party will retain or lose office at an election. But even if voting has this unique and crucial status, one should not misestimate its direct influence on the determination of government expenditure and taxation policies. The things to keep in mind in assessing the place of voting in the political process have been set out in chapter 3 in the discussion of the institutional framework. It is sufficient to recall here that in view of the fact that voting takes place at periods that can be as far apart as two, four, five, or even seven years, the other political activities will, on a day-to-day basis, be more dominant influences on government expenditure and taxation policies than voting, though voting will still be important for the reason given above.

2. Political Participation

This section begins with the assumption that the degree of coercion for an individual j must exceed a certain positive threshold—call it $\delta_j^* > 0$—before he engages in political activities. Throughout I assume that δ_j^* is a constant, but the generality of the present discussion is not impaired by this restriction.[2]

Given δ_j^*, the central argument of this section can be stated formally as follows: for a given level of costs, participation in political activities by citizen j is related to the difference between his desired or equilibrium position and his actual or experienced state—a difference which, as we have seen, is closely related to the degree of coercion δ_j. A citizen will participate in the political process, that is, will try to persuade the governing party to alter some of its policies (or he will oppose that party in view

2. For a discussion of the effect of thresholds on some choices, see N. E. Devletoglou, "Threshold and Rationality," *Kyklos* 21, Fasc. 4 (1968), pp. 623–36, and the literature cited in that paper.

of achieving the same objective), if $\delta_j > 0$, provided also that $\delta_j > \delta_j^*$. On the other hand, that citizen will support the governing party and therefore will not engage in political activities if $\delta_j = 0$ or if $\delta_j < \delta_j^*$ *and if he can assume that the other citizens behave like himself.*

This last provision must be emphasized since it provides another motivation for engaging in political action; furthermore, it is one that operates for all activities, though I will only return to it in the discussion of voting in section 9 below. If $\delta_j = 0$, citizen j is satisfied with the governing party's budget of policies and hence supports that party; there is nothing in this situation to lead him into action as long as action is costly since by definition he is satisfied. If, however, that citizen thinks that other citizens could, by their actions, force the governing party to change the bundle of policies in a way which would coerce him, he will himself engage in activities to support the government in maintaining the existing bundle. In other words, the basic interdependence of joint consumption, which is the most essential feature of public and non-private goods, will prompt some of those citizens who are not positively coerced by public policies to engage in political action if these citizens expect that the action of others will lead the government to implement policies that they do not like.

Stated differently, citizens will engage in political action if, given the costs of such action, they are coerced by the policies of the governing party or if they expect to be, an expectation which is related to their estimate of the behavior of other citizens and of the governing party's response to that behavior.[3]

In the discussion that follows, I assume that $\delta_j > 0$ and that

3. A different, but relevant, argument can be found in G. Garvey, "The Theory of Party Equilibrium," *American Political Science Review* (March 1966) pp. 29–39.

$\delta_j > \delta_j{}^*$, so that citizens engage in political activities aimed at supporting, opposing, or altering the expenditure and taxation policies of governing parties. I, further, make the expository assumption in discussing each activity that it is the only one that a citizen can choose; only in the next chapter do I examine the question of the choice between political activities.

3. Large Pressure Groups

Should the policies pursued by a government coerce some citizens, they would *not* join large pressure groups and lobbies in an effort to change that situation, for, as Olson has conclusively shown, pressure groups and lobbies are the by-products of large organizations that perform some non-pressure and non-lobbying functions for which they receive the support of their members; they would not otherwise exist.[4] It will be useful if Olson's central theme is briefly summarized. For an example, consider the case of the American Medical Association (A.M.A.). This large organization sometimes acts as a lobby and from time to time obtains changes in actual or proposed government policies. These changes are in the nature of collective or public goods and as such accrue to all medical doctors whether they are members of the A.M.A. or not. This being the case, each medical doctor would find it in his own interest not to pay his membership fees and other dues to the Association; since all doctors would react in the same way, the A.M.A. would wither away. The Association can obtain the support—and the fees—of medical doctors either through the use of force and repression or through the provision of private goods and services which the doctors want and need. As Olson

4. M. Olson, Jr., *The Logic of Collective Action* (Cambridge: Harvard University Press, 1965).

(and Kessel) has shown, the A.M.A. uses both methods and in so doing maintains an organization which can *then* act as a lobby and a pressure group.[5]

It follows that medical doctors do not decide to join the A.M.A. because government policies put them in a state of coercion, but because the A.M.A. can and does use force to maintain its membership and because it provides its members with a number of useful private and individual services which they would lose were they to leave the Association.[6] Since Olson's theory appears unassailable,[7] the question of the role of lobbies and interest and pressure groups in the political process must be examined anew.[8] If individuals do not join pressure groups as a result of coercion, what is it that they do—if they

5. R. A. Kessel, "Price Discrimination in Medicine," *The Journal of Law and Economics* (October 1958) pp. 20–53.

6. Olson also discusses the case of other organizations, some of which act as pressure groups and some which do not, and in all cases his theory possesses the same basic power.

7. R. Wagner in "Pressure Groups and Political Entrepreneurs," *Papers on Non-Market Decision Making*, ed. G. Tullock, (Charlottsville, va: University of Virginia Press, 1966) pp. 161–70 accepts Olson's theory, though he claims that its applicability is not general, because (1) there are other political activities besides pressure groups, and (2) "various market institutions often emerge to promote individual interest when individual rationality prevents group formation" (pp. 166–67). Both these points are well taken and neither Olson nor anyone else, I think, would seriously quarrel with them, though I do not think that Wagner's second point about the general emergence of market institutions is at all obvious and it is certainly not well documented. Wagner himself is able to cite only one case, H. G. Manne's "Mergers and the Market for Corporate Control," *Journal of Political Economy* (April 1965) pp. 110–20.

8. There is a large literature on the orthodox theory of pressure groups. Among the more famous, one can note J. R. Commons, *The Economics of Collective Action* (New York: Macmillan, 1951), pp. 23–35; D. B. Truman, *The Governmental Process* (New York: Knopf, 1951). When I wrote "A Theory of the Demand for Public Goods," *Canadian Journal of Economics and Political Science* (November 1966), pp. 455–67, I had not yet read Olson and consequently adopted the orthodox view of pressure groups.

do something—in relation to pressure groups and lobbies? The answer that I wish to suggest here is that the activities, recommendations, and demands of individuals within the large organizations which support lobbies are determined by the nature of the coercion engendered by the actual or potential implementation of particular government policies. To put it differently, Olson's theory provides us with a basic rationale for the existence of lobbies and pressure groups, but it does not tell us why these groups support some policies and oppose or combat others; I suggest that the specific activities of lobbies are determined by the extent of coercion felt by the individual members of the organization. Suppose, for example, that a government decides to implement a certain policy and that this decision puts 60 percent of the members of an organization supporting a lobby in a position of disequilibrium exceeding their threshold—that is $\delta > \delta^*$ for 60 percent of the members. If the organization operates on a simple majority decision-rule, it will oppose the policy if $\delta > 0$ for 60 percent of the members and support the policy and thus remain inactive if $\delta_j = 0$ for 60 percent of the members; it will remain inactive as long as it can assume that countervailing forces will not try to determine the government's decision.

To summarize, members of large organizations that support lobbies will try to influence the activities of their lobby in such a way as to improve their own position. Whether they will be successful in that endeavor will depend to a large extent on the decision-rule within the organization and, as the foregoing example illustrates, on the degree to which preferences of members are similar; therefore, one would expect such organizations as the A.M.A. to be more efficient as lobbies than labor unions, and lobbies of producers to be more efficient than those of consumers, since the tastes of M.D.'s and those of producers are certainly more homogeneous than those of workers and of consumers.

I have not in the above discussion indicated the instruments that lobbies can use to promote their aims. It is impossible to enumerate all these various instruments, but it may be useful to point out a few of them without giving any of them undue emphasis. Lobbies will try to bribe politicians directly with money or with things money can buy or indirectly by promoting the interest of persons who have the support of politicians. Lobbies can, if it is too difficult to convince politicians of a given point of view, try to convince some members of the electorate in the hope that these latter, once convinced, will influence the politicians. Lobbies often find it easier to influence the political process if a number of their executive members are former politicians or former high-ranking bureaucrats and consequently hire a number of these people. As a final illustration, lobbies may sue the government in an effort to achieve judicial redress if it is felt that governments engage in activities detrimental to the welfare of the lobby's members.

4. Individual and Small Group Activities

Many citizens are not, however, members of large organizations supporting a lobby; this does not mean that they cannot engage in political activities and bring pressure to bear on politicians. They can act individually and/or as members of small pressure groups. In both capacities they have a variety of instruments which they can use as the following illustrates: they can write letters directly to politicians or to newspapers, make representations, exert influence on others by word of mouth, deliver speeches pro or con on given policy, give financial and/or other support to political action groups, give funds to finance election campaigns, buy drinks, meals, furniture, vicuna coats for the relevant politicians, provide an opening for a friend or for a friend of a friend, give a promise of future help, and a host of other things.

The activities of small groups will tend to be widespread and thus can have an important influence on politicians for two main reasons. First, these activities are basically inexpensive to organize (though the sums involved may sometimes be important) since the number of individuals participating in any one of them is usually relatively small; and second, in view of the fact that preferences within a group are likely to be fairly homogeneous because of small numbers and also because small groups are often able to bypass the "free-rider" problem, they tend to be efficient in achieving their goals.[9]

One must certainly include among the individual and small group activities the activities of "old boys clubs," which tend to be especially prominent features of élitist societies. Since most of the pressures and influence exerted through these clubs are indirect and polite, they are more difficult to pinpoint and to trace than the more cut-and-dried pressures described above, but that does not imply that they are less real or less efficient.

For historical reasons one should probably point out two goals which have occupied pressure groups or which political theorists and moralists have claimed to be essential goals of pressure groups if democracy is to be real and strong. They are the popular recall of deputies or representatives as advocated by Proudhon and enshrined in the constitutions of many American states and more formally in that of the U.S.S.R., and the advocacy and building of new jurisdictions, that is, of political units larger or smaller than existing ones, to achieve a pattern of policies different from the existing one. In our time

9. The median size of small pressure groups in the United States is between 24 and 50 and a large number have less than twenty members. See E. E. Schattschneider, *The Semi-Sovereign People* (New York: Holt, Rinehart, and Winston, 1960), pp. 31–36.

the most important goal of this type has probably been that of creating a United States of Europe.

Organizing the popular recall of deputies is not an easy task, but if achieved it can lead to less coercion in that the removal of a politician who has departed substantially from the platform on which he was elected but still has many years in office, and his replacement by a more reliable one, will imply the removal of policies which generated coercion and their replacement by some that generate less. The creation of new jurisdictions will achieve the goal of less coercion in a different way. If the desire is for a larger unit, the presumption must be that some policies are either not supplied or not in sufficient amount either because the spillovers from the policies remain unpaid for or because the scale of production for these policies is too limited in each of the small units. If the desire is for new, smaller political units, the presumption must be that in smaller units, citizens are more able to supervise and control what is supplied to them than in larger units. In both cases the achievement of the goal means less coercion.

5. Social Movements

The activities described above are in effect permanent features of the political process; the one examined in this section does not have the same permanency. Indeed, one of its important characteristics is that it tends to be transitory, but recurrent. This activity I call participation in social movements. As I will attempt to show, these movements are the external mani-festation of coercion imposed on some citizens and leading to a demand for changes in public policies.

Social movements always involve a relatively large number of individuals; in terms of the argument developed in the previous chapter this means that a large number of individuals are coerced roughly at the same time, so much so that the presumption must be that the coercion results from a structural or environmental phenomenon. This is indeed the hypothesis adopted, and as a consequence in the remainder of this section I will restrict the discussion to a class of aggregate phenomena capable of generating coercion and hence a demand for social and political change in a large number of individuals and I will briefly indicate the type of response that such a demand is likely to stimulate.[10]

Consider a group of citizens who hold more or less definite plans about their career prospects, their income profiles, and their expenditure streams. All these plans must have been formulated by citizens making assumptions about their own behavior and about that of the environment. In other words, I assume that career, income, and expenditures are taken by citizens to be determined by two sets of forces: one personal and the other environmental. The first set is, by definition, under the control of citizens and therefore unlikely to change in unexpected ways or to affect all members of the group at once; not so with environmental forces: a change in these forces will in all likelihood not be foreseen by citizens so that it will of necessity bring about unexpected changes in career, income, and/or expenditure plans.

Suppose that we summarize the full environment by a single index such as the rate of growth of real social (national or regional) income per head; imagine now that a significant reduction in that rate of growth manifests itself and that this persists for a significant length of time.[11] As a result, the initial

10. This section summarizes a more detailed discussion of the same question in A. Breton and R. Breton, "An Economic Theory of Social Movements," *American Economic Review* (May 1969), pp. 198–205.

11. Both the size of the reduction in the rate of growth of social income and the length of time over which it must be sustained to have the required effect have to be decided on empirical grounds and will depend on the problem on hand; hence the quotation marks in the text.

plans of citizens will become unrealizable, and all will know that this situation has been caused by environmental factors since by assumption the contribution of personal factors has not changed or any changes in them are fully known to each citizen. What is important about the effect of a protracted reduction in the rate of growth of real income is that all the members of the group or of the collectivity are thereby coerced, though they need not be coerced to the same extent. This can be seen with the help of figure 5.1, which portrays the situation of one citizen or of a group of identical citizens. In that figure $Y(t)$ and $Y'(t)$ are two income streams, the former representing the situation prior to the (protracted) reduction in the rate of growth of social income, and $U(t)$ is the consumption stream. At time t_0 the individual is accumulating debts at a rate of AC/t_0A per unit of time in such a way that at t_1 he has accumulated ABC to be repaid at t_2; BDE is therefore equal to ABC plus interest

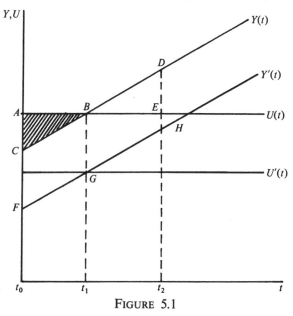

FIGURE 5.1

charges. If income prospects change from $Y(t)$ to $Y'(t)$, the individual can adjust his consumption downward to t_1G, for example, and still accumulate a total amount ABC of debt, which in terms of $Y'(t)$ $[<y(t)]$, however, represents a larger debt burden; he may therefore choose to reduce his consumption to something less than t_1G. The idea that he could sustain the same consumption level as he did at t_1B by borrowing AHF is difficult to imagine for most, if not all, citizens if only because the time-horizon of income streams will usually not extend sufficiently far in the future to make the repayment of larger debt and higher interest charges a sure enough gamble to induce lenders to advance the necessary funds.

Whatever happens, note that the welfare of citizens will have been affected adversely and since they have not engineered that change themselves, it coerces them; observe also that the extent of the damage is related to the expectation about income and consumption flows—the basic determinant of the size of the debt—and is therefore likely to vary between citizens. We now assume that this coercion imposed on citizens by the environment engenders a desire to redress the situation, a desire that can be called a demand for social and political change. This desire for redress or demand for social and political change will give rise to possibilities of monetary and non-monetary profits and the chances of political support which ad hoc political and social entrepreneurs as well as the elected representatives and contending political parties will want to reap. Indeed, if for one reason or another political parties do not respond fast enough to the demand for change by adopting the proper mix of public policies, social and political entrepreneurs will appear to reap these profits and the accompanying political support and in the process will supply social movements in the form of organized activities, new political ideologies, and promises of change.

If the demand for social change is large enough, if the lags in the political process are sufficiently long, and if, in addition, opposition or contending parties are weak or almost nonexistent, social and political entrepreneurs will be able to create large and important social movements which can lead to the appearance of third political parties; if opposition parties are strong, a period of civil disobedience, social upheaval, industrial strikes and unrest, chaos, and/or violence will be followed by changes in government policies taking place presumably at the margin.[12]

6. Individual Economic Adjustment

In the traditional literature of public finance, once the discussion of public goods and government expenditure is terminated and one moves ahead to the more familiar problems of excess-burden, shifting and incidence, and to the other adjustments which result from the imposition of taxes, it is habitual to forget that public or non-private goods exist and to proceed to the derivation of the theorems of taxation theory as if utility and production functions could be formulated exclusively in terms of private goods.

In the previous chapter a model was formulated which requires that taxation and expenditures be considered together. If we apply this model to the various possible adjustments of citizens to government policies, we reach the following conclusions. Considering first the effect of benefit taxes on the supply of effort (and of saving), we note that it can go either way depending on whether leisure (future private goods and services) is a substitute or a complement to public, non-private, and other private goods and services. To put if differently, the effects of

12. M. Pinard, "One-Party Dominance and Third Parties," *Canadian Journal of Economics and Political Science* (August 1967) pp. 358–73 and *The Rise of a Third Party*. (Englewood Cliffs, New Jersey: Prentice-Hall, 1971) discusses the role of the opposition in the appearance of social movements, albeit in a different framework than the one suggested here.

benefit taxes on the supply of labor (and of saving) are the same as that of any other price: with benefit taxes the magnitude of the effect depends on the sign and size of the cross-elasticity of the demand for leisure with respect to the appropriate tax, while in the case of any other good it depends on the sign and size of cross-elasticity of demand with respect to the price of the relevant product.

If benefit taxes were levied, the excess-burden of taxation would be zero because such taxes would reflect the marginal value placed on public and non-private goods by individual citizens. If the taxes levied are not benefit taxes—and in the previous chapter I have tried to show that, in the first instance at least, they will not be—excess-burden reappears, the incidence of the total budget becomes the proper focus of attention, and the incentive effects of taxes have to be studied in relation to actual and to desired expenditure policies. To illustrate, consider what would be the effects on the supply of labor of an excess (in terms of what is desired) provision of a public policy which of necessity would be accompanied by an excess sacrifice of a private good to pay for the policy, assuming an individual whose utility function is specified in terms of one private good, one public policy, and leisure. In that case if leisure and the private good are complements, but the private good and the public policy are substitutes, the supply of labor will be increased; if on the contrary the private good and the public policy are complements, it will fall. One could pursue the analysis by asking what would happen if the supply of public policies was less than the quantity desired, and so on for all possible situations. But the results need not be described since they are all implicit in the discussion of the previous chapter.

A basic point to remember, however, is that the adjustments which citizens make in the supply of efforts (and of saving) are channels through which they seek adjustment to coercive expenditure and tax policies. These may be as important as engaging in lobbying, pressure group activities, social movements, or participating in the other activities described above. In contrast to traditional analysis, however, I do not reach the conclusion that citizens *will* adjust to coercion in this way, only that they *may*; alternative ways are open to them between which they will choose.

This point becomes still more important if, in addition to private good, public policies, current and future goods, and leisure, we are careful to distinguish in the utility functions of citizens between those activities which are recorded by the tax authorities and those that are not, such as much of the after-hour labor of carpenters, painters, university teachers, or accountants. These nonrecorded activities make tax evasion a distinct possibility; furthermore, if we distinguish between legal and illegal activities, part of the adjustment to coercion will take the form of tax avoidance or of what is becoming known as "tax planning."

Through adjustment in individual activities citizens seek redress from coercion by altering their own behavior instead of trying to influence politicians. It must be observed, however, that their private behavior will have an indirect impact on the political process.[13] To clarify this, consider the case of labor supply. If, in response to coercion, a citizen decides to increase his consumption of leisure, he will by so doing reduce the tax base on which his tax liabilities are calculated, and since tax rates must initially be taken as given, he will thereby reduce the amount of revenue received by the government. If the level of government expenditure is constant—an assumption that could easily be relaxed—such behavior on his part will lead (since I assume no government borrowing) to higher tax rates for all

13.   See J. M. Buchanan, "Externality in Tax Response," *The Southern Economic Journal* (July 1966), pp. 35–42.

citizens, such that when applied to the new shrunken tax base, proceeds are sufficient to cover outlays. These higher tax rates will increase the extent of coercion imposed on many other citizens so that some who had not engaged in political action before will now do so, while others who were already participating in the political process will increase the intensity of that participation.

The external effect of regulating one's own private behavior in response to coercion, which in this case arose from the constant government expenditure constraint, could appear as a result of the collective consumption features of public and non-private goods. Private adjustments of the types just described have a public impact on the political process.

7. Private Provision

Governments supply a large number of public policies, but citizens do provide for themselves many goods and services with public goods elements. The reason is simple: governments may not make these goods available or, if they do, they may not provide them in sufficient quantities to eliminate coercion; fire protection was supplied privately by insurance companies in many parts of the world before being provided publicly, directional signs on roads in the U.K. are often provided by the Royal Automobile Club, and private charity still exists even though welfare state governments engage in income transfers.

In analyzing the private provision of public and non-private goods, it is useful to distinguish between the private supply which is done within the framework of the law and that which is illegal since engaging in the latter will usually be much more costly and as a consequence the institutional arrangements through which supply takes place will have a number of peculiar features.[14] Private provision that is legal can also take many forms—few of which have been studied by economists—and it would be pointless to describe them here, but these arrangements, being voluntary, will often lead to a reduction in the degree of coercion imposed by governments.[15] This can be examined in figure 5.2, a slightly modified version of figure 4.1.

Suppose that the amount of the public good provided by the government is S_0—which could obviously be at the origin—and suppose that at a tax-price of $\bar{q}$ per unit (equal to the marginal cost of S) the amount desired by A is $S_A{}^*$, which in figure 5.2 is less than S_0, and the amount desired by B is $S_B(> S_0)$. In such circumstances A will certainly not privately provide more of S, but if B can increase the supply of S at a price of $\bar{q}$ per unit, he will do so until the amount provided is $S_B{}^*$. If S_0 was at the origin, A and B could get together and, again holding to the assumption of a constant $\bar{q}$, they could collectively and privately provide up to $S_A{}^*$ at a price to each of $1/2\ \bar{q}$, after which B would have to proceed alone to provide $S_B{}^*$ at $\bar{q}$ per unit.

If S_0 was at the origin, however, the assumption of an equal price of $1/2\ \bar{q}$ for each citizen is not at all obvious, since cooperation could lead to private tax-prices adjusted to each indivi-

14. See S. Rottenberg in "The Clandestine Distribution of Heroin Its Discovery and Suppression," *Journal of Political Economy* (January–February 1968), pp. 78–90.

15. Buchanan, however, has analyzed one type of arrangement which prevails in some situations. See his "An Economic Theory of Clubs," *Economica* (February 1965), pp. 1–14. Some work has also been done on the theory of philanthropy. See in particular Boulding, "Notes on a Theory of Philanthropy"; Vickrey, "One Economist's View of Philanthropy," especially pp. 40–55. Also Kolm, "La production optimale de justice sociale"; C. M. Lindsay, "Medical Care and the Economics of Sharing," *Economica* (November 1969), pp. 351–62. Finally Mancur Olson, Jr., *The Logic of Collective Action*, chapter 1, has provided us with the conditions under which some public goods will be supplied by small groups.

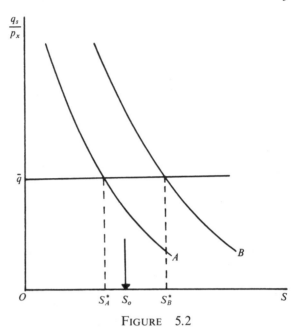

FIGURE   5.2

dual's marginal rate of substitution of S for X, the private good being used as the numéraire.

Often, of course, governments make the supply of certain private goods, such as narcotics or the operations of one's own stills, illegal. In these cases the foregoing analysis still applies though the unit price $\bar{q}$ must now include the concealment costs of reducing the probability of detection by the authorities, a magnitude which at the margin must be equal to the expected cost of being apprehended.

As with adjustments in one's own economic activities, private provision of public or non-private goods has an effect on the other members of the community. This is easily seen when citizens privately provide for themselves certain types of goods which it is illegal to provide since in these cases engaging in the illegal activity may cause harm to others. In general, as a look at figure 5.2 indicates, self-provision of public goods affects other citizens; as the figure shows, if B provides for himself S_B^* of S (at no cost to A, say), this quantity of the public good is also available to A. Whether A is better or worse off as a result of this will depend on a number of things which cannot conveniently be discussed within the limits of figure 5.2. If, for example, citizen B could deduct all or part of $\bar{q}(S_B^* - S_0)$—his own personal expenditures on S—from his tax base or from his taxes, he would in all probability indirectly increase A's tax-price or tax-share in the government's supply of other public policies. Similarly, if A thinks of S as a "bad" instead of as a good, one would have to conclude that B's private additional provision of S increases coercion on A since by definition in such a case the marginal utility of S to A would be negative.

8. Political Mobility

"Voting with one's feet" is an expression that well describes what is meant by political mobility. This activity, which has historically taken place on a wide scale, is also one through which citizens can seek to reduce some of the coercion that is placed on them.[16] Political mobility occurs when a citizen leaves a jurisdiction because the bundle of policies made available to him in it differs from the desired bundle and moves to another jurisdiction which supplies a set of policies that meets his preferences more closely. In other words, political mobility occurs when a citizen choses among jurisdictions the one "which best

16. Although seldom considered as policies, religious persecutions, racial discrimination and intolerance, political, economic and social ostracism, suppression of freedom, and other similar activities which governments sometimes carry out are policies in the sense given that term in chapter 2, hence the assertion in the text.

satisfies his preference pattern for public goods."[17]

This choice will be easier if, among other things, the number of jurisdictions between which citizens can choose is large and if the variance between the bundle of policies provided by jurisdictions is also large. It should be observed that the existence of political mobility as an instrument which can be used by citizens to reduce the coercion initially placed on them does not imply that the instrument will reduce coercion to zero for every citizen, even if removal and information costs were nil since, as just indicated, the number of jurisdictions and the variance between their policies must also be taken into account.[18] The fact that the instruments exist and can be used for the purpose described is all that matters here.

Like adjustments in one's private economic activities and self-provision, political mobility may have an effect on those who remain behind and thus affect the degree of coercion to which they are subjected. Given the interdependence between citizens consuming public policies, which for our purposes can be illustrated by the fact that the sum of the tax-prices paid by the J citizens of a jurisdiction must equal the marginal cost of producing the public policy, thus[19]

$$q^1 + q^2 + \cdots + q^j = c_i \qquad (5.1)$$

(where c_i is the marginal cost of amount S_0 of policy S_i and q^j

17. C. M. Tiebout, "A Pure Theory of Local Expenditures," p. 418. The question of political mobility has also been touched upon by H. C. Simons, *Economic Policy for a Free Society* (Chicago; University of Chicago Press, 1948), and G. J. Stigler, "The Tenable Range of Functions of Local Governments," Joint Economic Committee, *Federal Expenditure Policy for Economic Growth and Stability* (Washington, D. C.: Government Printing office, 1957), pp. 213–19.

18. See P. A. Samuelson, "Aspects of Public Expenditure Theories," *Review of Economics and Statistics* (November 1958), pp. 337–38.

19. Changes in the money supply and in borrowings being ruled out by assumption.

is the tax-price paid by citizen j), it follows that the departure of one individual must leave the burden of paying for policy i higher for all remaining citizens.

To expand upon this point, as long as c_i does not change—a situation that may obtain either because marginal cost is constant or, if marginal cost is rising or falling, because the quantity supplied remains unchanged—the departure of one or more citizens must increase the tax burden of all or of some of the others. Therefore, if a citizen who is remaining behind was initially in a state of equilibrium, the departure of another will lead to coercion which may or may not be large enough to exceed the threshold and prompt him to political action.

If the departure of an individual does not lead to increased tax burdens for the citizens remaining behind, it must lead to a reduction in the supply of public policies, a situation which is also conducive to increased coercion; whether these citizens will be led to react to this situation again depends on whether or not the increase in the degree of coercion exceeds or falls short of the individual's threshold.

The above discussion implicitly assumes that the coercion placed on a citizen is determined by forces that are unrelated to the level of his income; as a consequence, even if the departure of some citizens worsened (or improved) his income position, he would not act differently than I have described. This may often be a reasonable assumption to make. However, the analysis could be extended to take account of the effects of political mobility on the income of those remaining behind by examining the relationship between the amount of public policies desired and changes in their income. If public policies are not inferior goods, changes in income and changes in the amount of each policy desired will be in the same direction, while they will be in opposite directions if public policies are inferior goods. Changes in income will therefore lead to changes in the amount desired of public policies, and if the quantity actually supplied of these polcies does not change, they will lead to increases in the degree of coercion.

Whether the income of those remaining behind will increase or diminish when some citizens migrate is a complicated problem which has only recently been analyzed in general equilibrium terms.[20] It is not necessary to repeat this discussion here; suffice it to say that if the prices of the goods that are exchanged between jurisdictions can be assumed constant, political mobility and hence factor mobility (changing the factor endowment of a jurisdiction) will be consistent with constant factor prices as long as mobility does not lead the aggregate or social factor ratio to exceed or to fall short of the pre-mobility factor ratios in the various industries of that jurisdiction. If the prices of traded goods cannot be assumed not to change, variations in the income of citizens will depend in a crucial way on the demand for the goods produced in the jurisdiction.

9.   Voting

The discussion of voting can be fairly brief since much of the basic theory has been explored in some detail by other writers.[21] The central motivation is the same as for other activities: citizens vote to signal to the governing party that they are coerced, that is, that there exists a discrepancy between the set of policies that they desire and the one that is supplied. Should citizens be provided with exactly the bundle of policies that they

20.   H. G. Johnson, "Some Economic Aspects of Brain Drain," *The Pakistan Development Review* (Autumn 1967), pp. 379–411, especially the appendices.

21.   See, for example, Downs' *An Economic Theory of Democracy*. The motivation for voting in Downs' model is different from the one assumed here, but the discussion of the calculus of voting which he presents is fully applicable to my own model.

desire *and should they also assume that all other citizens are in the same position,* they would not vote.

Voting, like other activities, therefore, is a response to coercion or to expected coercion, the latter being related to an estimate of the behavior of other citizens and of the governing and contending parties' response to that behavior. Coercion would lead a citizen to oppose a party (or a candidate), while expected coercion would lead him to support it. However, in making a choice a utility-maximizing citizen will compare the degree of coercion and of expected coercion which the governing party imposes or could impose on him with the promises of the other parties. The comparison, it should be noted, is between actual performance and promises of performance, promises that do not relate to future policies, but to the current ones as these are written into law and implemented, modified by the knowledge that it is easier to make promises if they do not have to be realized immediately or in the near future.

If there is more than one opposition party, citizens, in addition to weighing the promises of the various parties, will make an estimate of how other voters are going to vote, and they may decide not to vote for the party which promises the smallest degree of coercion or of expected coercion, but in such a way as to keep the party they most dislike from being elected. They may even, if they discount the future at a low enough rate, vote for a party that promises to satisfy their preferences almost completely much later on, but has no chance of being elected now.

10. The Effective Set of Political Activities

For some citizens the instruments of political action examined above will be independent of one another, while for others they will either be complements or substitutes. Given this, the choice of instruments as well as the intensity with which they will be used will depend on the marginal cost of the activities compared with their expected marginal benefits. The last magnitude, as I have emphasized in the last chapter, is measured in terms of reductions in the extent of coercion felt by citizens, and therefore to preserve dimensional homogeneity the former magnitude must also be measured in subjective terms as the disutility resulting from the expenditures of money and time necessary to engage in political activities. If the marginal benefits of using a given instrument exceed its marginal cost *plus* some threshold, the activity will be chosen; if they do not, it will be left unused.

Within this framework the definition of complementarity and substitution is straightforward. If the marginal cost of instrument X falls and if instrument Y is then operated at a higher level of intensity, X and Y are substitutes; if Y had been operated at a lower level of intensity, X and Y would have been complements; with no change in the operation of Y, they would be independent of each other.

Before moving to the discussion of demand in the next chapter, I must emphasize that in addition to costs, returns, and threshold, there is another factor that will affect participation in the political process, namely, the knowledge or belief by some citizens that their preferences for policies are already correctly revealed by other citizens engaging in overt political activities, even though these last individuals may be completely unaware that they are doing this. In such cases participation in the political process would only take place if the citizens felt that the satisfaction of their preferences required more pressure to be brought on the governing party or if they thought that the citizens engaging in political action were not signaling their own preferences correctly. Political activities like the ones just described have many characteristics of public goods; they are, however, always provided privately.

6

The Demand for
Government Policies

1. Introduction

Chapter 4 discussed why citizens engage in political action and chapter 5 examined the various political activities or instruments which these same citizens can undertake or use in an effort to alter the amounts of public policies supplied by the government and thus bring them to levels that are more in accordance with their own preferences. This chapter focuses on the costs of engaging in the activities described in the last chapter and analyzes how political participation changes with changes in these costs. In effect, this chapter, building on the material of the last two, is intended to provide an institutional theory of the demand for public policies.

To develop this argument, I will, in the next section, analyze how political participation costs contribute to the level of political participation. Put differently, given the degree of coercion (and hence the bundle of tax and expenditure policies, as well as the utility functions and the money incomes of citizens), I will examine why a change in the costs of political participation will be accompanied by (1) a change in the kind of political instruments used by citizens and (2) a more intensive use of these

99

instruments.[1] Then I will examine how changes in the degree of coercion—resulting either from changes in the quantity of public policies supplied, in their tax-prices, in the preferences of citizens, or in their incomes—will alter the extent of political participation.

It may be well to emphasize even at this early stage that while changes in the vector of political participation costs for citizen $j(p_{ij}{}^*)$ (where i stands for the ith political instrument) permit the tracing out of a functional relationship between these costs and the degree of political participation, they do not provide us with a relationship between $p_{ij}{}^*$ and the level of expenditure and taxation policies separately. By implication we can establish that for a given level of tax parameters a reduction in $p_{ij}{}^*$ will lead to demands for larger expenditures, and for a given level of expenditures a fall in $p_{ij}{}^*$ will be accompanied by an increased demand for lower taxes. But when both types of policies are allowed to vary, we could observe an increased demand for lower or for higher expenditures and for lower taxation, though we should seldom observe increased demands for higher taxation, unless, of course, the tax bases are such that the higher would be borne by other citizens.

Sections 3 and 4 will examine the nature of political participation costs and analyze some of the factors that affect their height as well as how they vary. Section 5 discusses briefly the effect of alternative forms of political organizations on these costs and concludes that a federal structure, as a rule, is a form of political arrangement that tends to make political participation costs lower than other forms of political organization.

Before ending the chapter, I digress briefly on some features of communist regimes and conclude with a short, formal summary of the demand side of the model.

1. I also assume that the height of individual thresholds are given. See chapter 5, section 2.

2. The Use of Political Instruments

The various instruments of political action described in chapter 5 are not used by citizens unless these latter feel that they are coerced by government behavior or unless they believe that the use of the same instruments by other citizens will lead to the implementation of policies that would ultimately coerce them. Actual or expected coercion therefore provide us with the fundamental rationale for political action. Coercion, as we have seen, can be reduced or eliminated or forestalled by operating on the supply of public policies. It is, therefore, the desire to act on the supply of government output which makes it necessary for citizens to make use of the instruments of political action. In formal economic terms this means that the desire to use one or more of the political instruments gives rise to a derived demand for them, a demand derived from the demand for public policies.

The factors that determine the shape of the derived demand curve for political instruments—that is, the elasticity of the curve at any point—are the elasticity of the technocratic demand curve for a given public policy; the elasticity of substitution between a given political instrument (or activity) and other instruments (or activity), that is, the percentage change in the ratio in which instruments are used when there is a percentage change in the ratio of their costs to the user; and, finally, the fraction of the total cost of using political instruments accounted for by a given instrument.[2]

To examine how political instruments are chosen by citizens, that is, to examine the effect of the three factors determining the shape of the derived demand function, assume that the use of

2. A. Marshall, *Principles of Economics*, 8th ed. (New York: Macmillan, 1920), Book V, chapter 6 especially pp. 385–86. Marshall's first and fourth conditions are here collapsed into one, the second one.

political instruments (or activities) does not yield any direct utility to the users. This is an assumption that simplifies the analysis, but it is not one that is essential to it. Second, assume that the use of any instrument requires market goods (money) and time inputs so that the cost of using a political instrument must be defined as the sum of the money and time inputs necessary to produce a reduction in coercion.[3] Third, assume that to reduce coercion by one unit each instrument requires a fixed money and a fixed time input or, to put it differently, requires that marginal market resource and time inputs are employed in constant proportion.

Having made these assumptions, we can denote the money

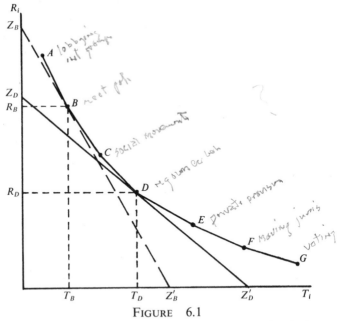

FIGURE   6.1

3. G. S. Becker, "A Theory of the Allocation of Time," *Economic Journal* (September 1965), pp. 493–517.

(or market resource) inputs as R_i and the time inputs as T_i, where $i = A, B, C, D, E, F, G$, standing for the seven instruments of political participation described in the previous chapter. If we arrange these instruments according to the increasing order of their time intensity and if we plot the resulting locus on a diagram, we trace a curve such as $A\ B\ C\ .\ .\ .$ in figure 6.1. This curve gives us the locus of factor proportions required to use the instruments of political action in such a way as to reduce the extent of coercion by one unit. $A\ B\ C\ .\ .\ .$ is therefore a production isoquant; one could plot any number of other isoquants to protray larger or smaller reductions in coercion.

On the iso-cost curve $Z_D Z_D{}'$, depicting the relative price of the two inputs, we observe that the citizen portrayed in figure 6.1 will use political instrument D. Note that since the price of time varies between night and day, week and weekend, summer and winter, mornings and afternoons, etc., it is possible for a citizen to use instrument D at one time and instrument B at another time when the price of the time input relative to that of the money input is higher as indicated by the iso-cost line $Z_B Z_B{}'$.

Even though each instrument of political action uses money an time inputs in fixed proportion, it is possible, as political participation increases in intensity, for a given citizen to switch from one instrument to another. In figure 6.2 two citizens are assumed to use instrument D on $Z_1 Z_1{}'$ when only one unit of coercion-reduction is desired; when more is wanted, one citizen may keep on using D and then switch to C while the other switches to E, immediately then to F, as shown by the solid and the broken lines in the diagram. In other words, it cannot be assumed that the production functions are homogeneous.

In figure 6.1, I have assumed that political instruments use money and time inputs in different proportions; this need not be the case. If two instruments use factors of production in the

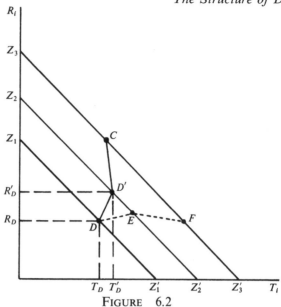

FIGURE   6.2

same proportion, a citizen could be observed using both in-struments—they would simply be used at different intensities then if only one instrument were used.

An increase in money income will generally lead to an increase in the price of time, hence one would expect higher income citizens to use political instruments (i.e., to engage in political activities) which are market-good intensive and lower income groups to use time-intensive instruments. Put another way, activities like lobbying, private provision, and some pressure-group behavior require relatively more market-resource inputs such as bribes, graft, monetary contributions to political parties and gifts to politicians, and also skilled personnel and per-manent secretaries that have to be paid and therefore should have a higher incidence among higher income groups, while activities such as social movements and some other pressure-group behavior require relatively more time-intensive inputs such as sit-ins and demonstrations and should therefore have a higher incidence in lower income groups.

Alternatively, even if the price of time is not related to income, but if the marginal productivity of money inputs is greater than that of time inputs, one would expect to observe higher income individuals use more of the money than of the time inputs and vice versa for the lower income persons.

It should be noted also that as long as the output of the public sector is not inferior, an increase in income will lead to an increased demand for public output; this, given the tax configuration existing before the increase in income, will lead to increased or reduced coercion and therefore to a desire for more or less political participation. The net effect of an increase in income on the demand for political instruments (i.e., on their use) will therefore be directly related to the size of the income elasticity of the demand for public output and inversely related to the cost (p_{ij}^*) [$= C_{Ri}R_i + C_{Ti}T_i$, where C_{Ri} and C_{Ti} are the costs of the money and time inputs respectively] elasticity of the demand for policy instruments. This last magnitude is, of course, related to the elasticity of the price of time with respect to income (I), i.e., to (dC_{Ti}/dI) (I/C_{Ti}), and to the time intensity of the political instrument used.

The analysis of the preceding paragraph can be applied mutatis mutandis to a change in the tax-price of public policies by recalling that the demand for these policies is inversely related to their tax-prices.

The foregoing discussion can be summarized and extended with the help of figure 6.3. To simplify the diagrammatic analysis, assume that it is possible to sum the costs of political participation p_{ij}^* over the J citizens and as a consequence one can write p_{ij}^* as p_i^* where i stands for the ith political instrument. Assume also that when S_1 of S is supplied, the tax-price is q_1, so that

Panel A

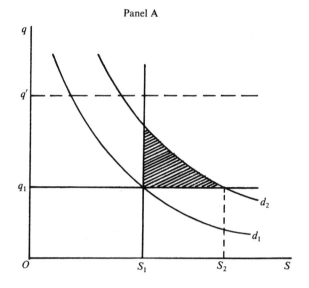

Panel B

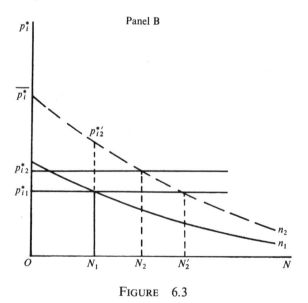

FIGURE 6.3

given the technocratic demand curve d_1 (for given preferences and income), the degree of actual coercion is zero. This is shown in panel A. Note that in panel B, the extent of political participation (N) when actual coercion is zero is not itself zero; the level of N at N_1 when p_i^* is p_{i1}^* reflects some degree of expected coercion, that is, reflects expectations about the behavior of other citizens; so do all other points on the n_1 curve.

Assume now that as a result of an increase in income, the technocratic demand curve shifts to d_2, the tax-price and the quantity of public output remaining unchanged. Coercion now is positive and is equal to the shaded area in panel A since with the demand condition reflected in d_2, the quantity of S now desired is S_2, while the quantity supplied is still S_1. The political participation curve shifts from n_1 to n_2 and participation increases from N_1 to N_2', assuming that p_i^* does not change. An increased income has increased political participation. N_2' does not, however, represent the equilibrium level of N since with the increase in income, the cost of political participation will also increase, let us say to p_{i2}^*; the equilibrium level of N will be N_2. Note that an increase in income could lead to a reduction in N if that increase raised p_i^* above p_{i2}^*.

All comparative statical displacement can be analyzed with the help of figure 6.3. For example, if the increase in income had led to a higher tax-price—such as q', say—the degree of coercion would have been equal to the triangle opposite the shaded one. Thereafter, one proceeds as above. If, to take another case, the initial supply of S had been S_2, an increase in income which had shifted demand to d_2 would have reduced the degree of actual coercion to zero and consequently shifted the political participation curve from n_2 to n_1 and p_i^* from p_{i2}^* to p_{i1}^*. As a last example, suppose that the increase in income pushed p_i^* above $\overline{p_i^*}$, then instrument i would not be used and either another instrument would be used or political participation would fall to zero.

Note finally that the shape of the political participation curves (n_1 and n_2) is determined by the factors analyzed above, that is, by the factors determining the shape of derived demand curves.

3. The Cost of Voting

This section and the next are intended to be non-rigorous discussions of the costs of political participation; they both aim at providing empirical substance to the abstract concept of political participation cost. Since voting is different from the six other activities described in the previous chapter, I devote the present section to it and then move on to the other instruments in the next section.

The costs of voting are to a large extent determined by the characteristics of the institutional framework of the public sector and in particular by the length of the election period. As already pointed out in chapter 3, during the time span between election days, the costs of voting are infinite in that no voting can take place during that period. In a figurative way, it is possible to say that the costs of voting vary with the length of the election period, even though, except on election days, they remain equal to infinity; this is because with shorter election periods the activity can effectively be engaged in more often, while with longer election periods that instrument must be more seldom used.

The fact that voting does not make it possible to discriminate between policies, but must usually be used to select one representative who may not turn out to be a member of the winning coalition, implies that per unit to output—i.e., per unit of reduced coercion—the costs are high. Moreover, decision-rules which place some citizens in a permanently losing coalition, make the cost of reductions in coercion high. It should come as no surprise, therefore, that other instruments have come to be used to influence politicans and are now permanent features of democratic societies. The rationale for lobbies, pressure groups, social movements, political mobility, etc., is to be found in the basic characteristics of the institutional framework and in the cost that it imparts to voting. Should the decision-rule be unanimity, the length of the election period zero, full-line supply abolished, and other incidental costs to be examined presently set equal to zero, lobbies, pressure groups, etc., would wither away, and voting would be the only political instrument used to signal coercion and to achieve reductions in it.

When we turn to the costs of voting that have to be met on election day—the incidental costs to which allusion was made above—we note that for enfranchised individuals they are fairly low. In some countries the time costs are made even lower than they would otherwise be by laws requiring that election days be public holidays or by placing them on a Sunday.[4] In most countries, furthermore, the number of polling stations is large and their location is such that the money and time costs of traveling from one's residence to the place of voting and back are also low; in addition, transportation facilities are often provided free by political organizers wishing to make voting easier for those citizens who are expected to support their candidate or party.

But the costs of voting are not zero. In some instances a poll tax may exist, in others, residence and/or registration requirements that temporarily make the cost of voting infinite or higher than it would be are part of the basic rules. In addition, there are information costs, namely the costs of acquiring information on the bundle of policies proposed by all candidates and parties

4. In some countries (Australia and Belgium, for example) the cost of voting is made even lower by the existence of a tax levied on those who do not vote.

and on the reliability of politicians and parties. These costs are not negligible, though their magnitude should not be exaggerated.[5] Citizens can easily be assumed to know their preferences; whether they can be assumed to know the degree of coercion that is imposed on them and hence the pattern of tax-prices and public expenditures which together with their preferences and their incomes generates that coercion is basically the question facing us. Note that whether the citizens' knowledge is mistaken or not, whether it is complete or not, whether it is systematically biased or not has no bearing on the issue, at least for positive analysis.

I conclude that the high (prohibitive) cost of voting between election days tells us why citizens use other political instruments besides voting; and that the relatively low cost of voting on election days explains why so many people vote. Whether they cast their vote in a socially optimal fashion, that is, by taking all the socially relevant information into account, is an important question, but one which is normative in character and hence beyond the limits of this work.

4. The Cost of Political Participation

We have already seen that the costs of using the various instruments of political action can be divided into money and time costs. It may sometimes also help to distinguish between organization and communication (including transportation and information) costs. The first include the market goods and time inputs that have to be employed by a political entrepreneur to bring groups of citizens together to participate in one (or more) political activity (these costs could be called recruitment

5. Downs, *An Economic Theory of Democracy*, especially chapters 11–14. Tullock, *Toward a Mathematics of Politics*, especially chapters 7–9.

costs); they also include the money and time inputs required to keep these citizens organized in a cohesive and organic fashion so that the group will have some impact on politicians (bargaining costs); and finally, they include the outlays necessary to find the resources that will insure some stability and permanency to the group and some support for the activities that are conducive to the attainment of the goal or goals of the group (running costs).

Communication costs, on the other hand, are the money and time inputs that go into the acquisition and diffusion of information and knowledge about the preferences of citizens and about the coercion felt by these citizens (advertising and propaganda costs); they also include the inputs required to move from one jurisdiction to another, including the cost of acquiring information on the other jurisdictions (transport costs).

Organization and communication costs are certainly not independent of one another, especially in the long run. Indeed, the observable secular decrease in organization costs is to a large extent the product of changes in the technology of communication. But in the shorter run, one can say that organization costs vary: (1) positively with the size of the group organized, (2) inversely with the degree of homogeneity in the tastes of those organized, and (3) with the legality or illegality of the activity. Short-run communication costs in turn will vary: (1) with the presence or absence of political censorship or with the existence and height of barriers to movement, (2) positively with the size of jurisdictions, and (3) inversely with the degree of urbanization and with the diffusion of the mass media (radio, television, newspapers, telephones, but also automobiles, airplanes,e tc.).

It is of some value to note that the costs of the three political activities which affect politicians and political parties only indirectly (namely, the self-provision of public and non-private policies, political mobility, and adjustments in one's private activities) are of a slightly different character than the costs of the other activities (large lobbies, smaller pressure groups, and social movements) in that often—though certainly not always—the use of these instruments does not require the cooperation of others. This is surely the case with the last two mentioned activities, even if self-supply will sometimes only be possible with the cooperation of others; even in this case the costs often have to be met by each citizen alone.

Most of what can be said about the costs of political mobility and of self-supply is already known, but we may note that adjustments in the supply of labor or savings and/or changes in the structure of one's consumption budget or in the composition of one's portfolio as a result of a discrepancy between the desired bundle of public policies and the one that is actually provided all impose costs on citizens, costs that can be measured in money or in utility terms. These costs are in the nature of welfare losses and thus depend on the size of the elasticities of supply (labor and savings) and demand (goods and securities) functions and on the degree of coercion to which citizens are subjected.

By way of conclusion for this section, observe that if the costs of self-provision, individual adjustments, and political mobility are higher than the costs of operating lobbies, pressure groups, and social movements, the empirical incidence of the former relative to the latter will be low and as a consequence we would tend to observe mostly the latter to the near exclusion of the former. In other words, we would observe lobbies, pressure groups, and social movements, but no self-supply, individual adjustment, or political mobility. As things are, we observe lobbies, pressure groups, social movements, self-supply, some political mobility, but very little individual adjustment.[6] Indeed,

6. W. E. Oates, "The Effects of Property Taxes and Local Public

the studies we possess of the effect of taxes on the supply of labor all indicate that this effect is small or nonexistent.[7] In the present framework, this is not implausible. It would seem that to achieve the same degree of redress from coercion by using individual adjustment instead of the other instruments that act more directly on politicians, one would have to operate that instrument at very high levels and hence to pay high costs. The observed facts therefore seem to be consistent with the hypothesis of this study.

5.   Federalism and Participation Costs

While this is not the place to develop a theory of federalism, it will be useful, however, to point out that a federal structure affects both voting costs as these are determined by the in-

---

Spending on Property Values: An Empirical Study of Tax Capitalization and the Tiebout Hypothesis," *Journal of Political Economy* (November–December 1969), pp. 957–71.

7. T. H. Sanders, *Effects of Taxation on Executives* (Cambridge: Harvard University Press, 1951); R. Davidson, "Income Taxes and Incentive: The Doctors' Viewpoint," *National Tax Journal* (September 1953) pp. 293–97; G. F. Break, "Income Taxes, Wage Rates and the Incentive to Supply Labor Services," *National Tax Journal* (December 1953) pp. 333–52; "Effects of Taxation on Incentives," *British Tax Review* (June, 1957) and "Income Taxes and Incentives to Work," *American Economic Review* (September 1957) pp. 529–49; H.M.S.O., *Royal Commission on Profits and Income* (Cmnd 9105, 1954) p. 108; S. E. Rolfe and G. Furness, "The Impact of Changes in Tax Rates and Method of Collection on Effort: Some Empirical Observations," *Review of Economics and Statistics* (November 1957) pp. 394–401; J. N. Morgan, M. H. David, W. J. Cohen, and H. E. Brazer, *Income and Wealth in the United States* (New York: McGraw-Hill, 1962) pp. 76–77; H. G. Grubel and D. R. Edwards, "Personal Income Taxation and Choice of Professions," *Quarterly Journal of Economics* (February 1964) pp. 158–63; and R. Barlow, H. E. Brazer, and J. N. Morgan, *Economic Behaviour of the Affluent* (Washington: Brookings Institution, 1966), p. 38.

stitutional framework and the level of other political participation costs in a way that makes the representation of the preferences of citizens easier. To understand how federalism alters voting costs, let me define federalism as a political system in which the responsibility for providing public policies to citizens is distributed—by a constitution—over different levels of elected governments. As a consequence, if we are given a list of functions to be performed by the public sector, the introduction of a federal structure to replace a unitary one will immediately increase the number of representatives who have to account for those policies. Since these representatives will be elected in different jurisdictions, the control or power of citizens over policies is also increased. To grasp this, imagine that in a given jurisdiction made up of 100 citizens, 60 favor policy S_1 while 40 want S_2 and assume that as a result of this S_1 is implemented, a conclusion that follows if voting is based on a simple majority rule and is exercised on the policy itself and not on representatives. Suppose now that the jurisdiction is broken in two and that each new jurisdiction (J_1 and J_2) has 50 citizens; further, that in J_1 30 citizens favor S_2 and 20 support S_1. Since we are dealing with the same population as before, in J_2 40 citizens must favor S_1, while 10 must favor S_2. As a result, J_2 will implement S_1 and J_1, S_2, so that while under the unitary structure 60 percent of the citizens had their preferences satisfied, in the federal system 70 percent now have theirs satisfied.[8]

An argument which leads to the same basic conclusion can be devised for any decision-rule as well as for any of the combination of decision-rules which exist in representative democracies. But that is not all. A federal system as compared to a unitary one reduces the freedom of politicians to combine policies in bundles, which, though acceptable to citizens, are far from those

---

8. J. R. Pennock, "Federal and Unitary Government-Disharmony and Frustration."

that maximize their welfare, that is, it reduces the extent of full-line supply. To see this, it is sufficient to recognize that in a two-party system a citizen will vote for the party that promises to implement policy S_1 for which he has a strong preference, even though he will have to accept S_2 which he doesn't like, but for which his dislike is small. In a federal structure, that citizen will still be able to support the party promising S_2 at another level.

Federalism thus reduces the extent of full-line supply, but it does not eliminate it altogether for as long as politicians are able to obtain electoral support by implementing policies which citizens desire and coupling them with other policies that may be positively disliked by up to 100 percent of the electorate, full-line supply will exist. But ceteris paribus the respect for individual preferences is greater in federal structures since the possible trading of policies is reduced by the fact that politicians at each level have fewer policies to trade.

A federal structure also has an influence on the other costs of political participation. While it must be recognized that influencing political parties at many levels of government is costlier than influencing only one, all the other consequences of federalism are to reduce (or at least not to increase) the costs of using the instruments of political participation.[9] The increase in the number of jurisdictions which follows upon the introduction of federalism automatically reduces the costs of moving from one jurisdiction to another and thus makes the choice of the jurisdiction that provides the desired bundle of goods or at least certain goods that have high weights —such as schools for citizens with school-going children—an easier task than it would otherwise be. The costs of adjusting

9. It is most certainly for that reason that American Blacks have chosen to act on the federal government, instead of on state governments, a phenomenon that was helped by the fact that in some states they were *in practice* not franchised.

one's own personal economic activity are not altered by the introduction of a federal structure, but the costs of organizing the private provision of public and non-private policies, the costs of organizing lobbies, pressure groups, and social movements will be reduced, if for no other reason than that of the reduction in the size of jurisdictions. But these costs will also be reduced because with the reduction in the costs of moving, the preferences of the population in each jurisdiction will be more homogeneous and hence organization costs will be lower. It is not an accident, therefore, that local politicians are closer to the people than are national politicians, but only a reflection of the fact that the costs of signaling individual preferences are lower in federal structures than in unitary ones.

6. A Digression on Communist Regimes

Even if this study deals only with decision-making and resource allocation in democratic societies, it is instructive to look at communist regimes for the light they shed on the working of the public sector in democracies. In all communist societies, periodic elections take place though political parties are not allowed to compete with one another.[10] What is more interesting,

10. Interestingly enough the technique of voting in the U.S.S.R. deprives voters of the power that voting usually gives to citizens and explains why 99% or so of the electorate supports the candidate whose name appears on the ballot. The technique is as follows: if a voter wants to support the candidate on the ballot he simply folds the ballot in view of everyone in the polling station and drops it in a box provided for that purpose. If, however, he does not wish to support the candidate, he must strike his name off the ballot by entering a booth, then return to the box and deposit his ballot. Anyone who enters the booth, therefore, is known to all present not to have supported the candidate. This even if voting is, by constitution, secret in the U.S.S.R. See J. M. Gilison, "Soviet Elections as

however, is that the use of all (but one) of the political instruments described in the last chapter is illegal, avowedly because these instruments are decadent and bourgeois, though the consequence of this is to remove all demand considerations from the determination of public output. Lobbies, pressure groups, social movements (even labor unions), private provision, and political mobility (the so-called iron or bamboo curtains) are all illegal. In most instances a citizen engaging in these activities is punished by hard labor or by death. As a consequence, the costs of using these instruments are very high. It is interesting to note that it is almost impossible to regulate or effectively outlaw adjustments at the level of a citizen's own economic activity, though repeatedly in the history of the U.S.S.R. and of the People's Republic of China there have been efforts to punish anyone using that instrument. But policing such "diktats" is not easy and therefore it should not be surprising that observers of communist societies have often reported an intense use of that activity; observers have reported that the population was not working as hard as it could, was not saving any money and that the level of thievery (sometimes also punishable by hard labor or by death) was very high.

That the reforms of recent years across communist Eastern Europe and Russia are avowedly all oriented toward reducing the use of that instrument give strength to the above observations. If the analysis developed in this study is valid and if communist regimes do not lower the costs of using other instruments of political action—what the Czechoslovakia of Mr. Dubcek was undoubtedly trying to do before the Russians intervened—I would conjecture that all current reforms are headed for complete failure. Success for these reforms can only

---

a Measure of Dissent: The Missing One Per Cent," *American Political Science Review* (September 1968).

result from reducing the costs of using other political instruments or of otherwise eliminating coercion.[11]

7. A Brief Formal Summary

It is possible at this point to summarize formally the argument of this and the two previous chapters. In chapter 4, I derived a technocratic function relating the quantity demanded of a policy to its tax-price and to the income of citizens.[12] For a given citizen j, this relationship [equation (4.11) of chapter 4] can be written as

$$S^j = F^j(q^j, I^j) \qquad (j = 1, \ldots J) \qquad (6.1)$$

where S^j is the quantity of the public expenditure policy S demanded by j, q^j is the tax-price facing j, and I^j is his money income.

We also saw that

$$\frac{\partial F^j}{\partial q^j} < 0 \qquad (6.2)$$

and that

$$\frac{\partial F^j}{\partial I^j} \lessgtr 0 \qquad (6.3)$$

In the present chapter, we saw that the technocratic demand relationship represented as (6.1) can be transformed into an institutional demand relationship by introducing into (6.1) the

11. Since all public finance literature virtually assumes that the only instrument that can be used by citizens is adjustment in one's own economic activity, should one conclude that the basic political framework underlying that literature is dictatorship?

12. In this summary I neglect the relationship between policy bundles and tax shares that was discussed in chapter 4, section 4. The argument in the text can be easily modified for this alternative formulation of the problem.

vector of political participation costs, i.e., the vector of the costs of using the seven political instruments described in chapter 5. Thus,

$$S^j = G^j(q^j,\ I^j,\ p_{ij}{}^*) \quad i = 1,\ .\ .\ .,\ 7 \qquad (6.4)$$
$$j = 1,\ .\ .\ .,\ J$$

where $p_{ij}{}^*$ is the cost to citizen j of using the ith political instrument.

Though we know that the ith instrument will be used more intensely by citizen j when its cost falls, we do not know the sign of $\partial G^j/\partial p_{ij}{}^*$. The definition of the coercion in chapter 4 and the argument of that chapter and of the present one indicate that the sign of $\partial G^j/\partial p_{ij}{}^*$ will depend on the nature of the coercion felt by citizen j, that is, given q^j, on whether the amount of S already supplied by the government *exceeds* or *falls short* of the amount desired. Therefore,

$$\frac{\partial G^i}{\partial p_{ij}{}^*} \lessgtr 0 \qquad (6.5)$$

If we wish to sum the demand functions (6.4) over all citizens, we could first write

$$S = \sum_j^J S^j \qquad (6.6)$$

and

$$I = \sum_j^J I^j \qquad (6.7)$$

and define Q to be the vector of all q^j and $p_i{}^*$ the vector of all participation costs for instrument i. We would have

$$S^d = g(Q, I, p_i{}^*) \qquad (6.8)$$

where the superscript d to S has been added to indicate that (6.8) is a demand function.

In concluding, let me suggest that the statistical studies that have regressed government expenditures on tax rates (or tax-shares) however defined, without including p_i^* (or a proxy) among the explanatory variables and have nevertheless found a stable (measured by a t- or F-test) relationship between these expenditures and Q have accidentally hit upon a set of data from a universe in which p_i^* ($i = 1$), . . . 7 was low. Had p_i^* been high—as was no doubt the case for other sets of data—no relationship between expenditures and Q would have been measured though one could have been found if p_i^* had been included in the analysis. Other factors, however, are at work in the public sector and we should not, therefore, expect to understand too much by looking exclusively at the demand side of that sector.

III

The Structure of Supply

. . . I know that everyone will admit that it would be highly praise-worthy in a prince to possess all the above named qualities that are reputed good but as they cannot all be possessed or observed, human conditions not permitting of it, it is necessary that he should be prudent enough to avoid the scandal of those vices which would lose him the state, and guard himself if possible against those which will not lose it him, but if not able to, he can indulge them with less scruple. And yet he must not mind incurring the scandal of those vices, without which it would be difficult to save the state, for if one considers well, it will be found that some things which seem virtues would, if followed, lead to one's ruin, and some others which appear vices result in one's greater security and wellbeing.

N. Machiavelli

. . . the doctrine that statesmen must always act contrary to their convictions, when to do otherwise would lose them office, implies that they are less easily replaceable than is really the case.

J. M. Keynes

7

The Behavior of Political Parties

1. Introduction

In chapter 4, it seemed reasonable or at least consistent with tradition to assume without justification that citizens maximize utility functions in which, in addition to private goods, government policies (of a public and private goods variety) enter as variables; the hypothesis that governing and opposition (i.e., non-governing) political parties (and politicians) maximize a utility function defined for a probability of reelection (or election) variable—and for other variables as well, as I will indicate below and examine in more detail in chapter 10—however needs explanation and defense. The present chapter, therefore, discusses the hypothesis in some detail, though the full implications of its meaning will only be known at the end of chapter 11 when it has been used to produce results.

In addition, even if the governing party and the opposition—the whole group of politicians—play an important role on the supply side of the public sector, there is no doubt that bureaus also have an influence on supply. For that reason, after the discussion of the behavior of the governing party in this chapter and of the technical conditions that constrain that behavior in the next, I will, in chapter 9, examine the hypothesis that bureaucrats seek to maximize the relative size of their bureaus.

Both these hypotheses about politicians and bureaucrats, but especially the first one, represent radical departures from the hypotheses that intellectuals (and among them economists) and politicians themselves have entertained about the behavior of political parties and governments. The traditional view is that politicians seek *the* common good, *the* public interest, or *the* welfare of society though these terms have seldom, if ever, been defined in an empirically meaningful way. If one, however, adopts an intuitive definition of the common good, the public interest, or the social welfare, a hypothesis which incorporates them does not appear very productive of empirically relevant propositions and in particular seems to account for very little of what governments in fact do. For that reason I simply discard this hypothesis and others of that class and adopt the ones suggested in the preceeding paragraphs.

2. The Governing Party

Let us therefore assume that each politician who is a member of a political coalition can be characterized by a utility function defined for a probability of reelection (or election) variable and for variables such as personal pecuniary gains, personal power, his own image in history, the pursuit of lofty personal ideals, his personal view of the common good, and others which are peculiar to each politician. We can write these utility functions as:

$$U_p' = U_p(\pi, a_m) \qquad (p = 1, \ldots P)$$
$$(m = 1, \ldots M) \quad (7.1)$$

where p stands for any given politician, π is the probability of reelection variable, and the a_m's are the variables just mentioned.

Equations (7.1) are to be maximized subject to some level of π—say π^*—below which that variable cannot be allowed to fall, lest the politicians be defeated at the polls, and subject to some technical conditions or constraints. Without a knowledge of these conditions or constraints, the hypothesis that political parties (and politicians) maximize (7.1) is not a very interesting one since the range of possible behaviors encompassed by the hypothesis is not restricted in any way and one can only conclude that politicians do what they do because doing so maximizes their utility. The problem is exactly similar to that encountered in the theory of the firm; there, entrepreneurs who are assumed to be maximizing profits (or a utility function defined for a profits variable only) are assumed to be constrained by technical conditions of production. The next chapter discusses the production conditions that constrain (7.1), but before I can engage in that exercise, two different problems must be examined: the first arises in defining the relevant decision-making unit, and the second in ascertaining the exact meaning that should be given to the concept of maximization itself.

The first problem can be stated differently. Above, I have assumed that each politician is characterized by a utility function such as (7.1) and hence implicitly assumed that decisions are made by individual politicians represented by a utility function such as (7.1). However, decisions in the public sector of democratic countries are not usually made by politicians acting alone; instead, these individuals tend to organize themselves in coalitions, sometimes coterminal with the frontier of the political party to which they belong, as is usually the case in parliamentary-type systems, sometimes not, as often happens in the American congressional system. Whatever the nature of the coalition, it is important to know how, as a coalition, the party arrives at a decision on any particular set of issues. This kind of question must always be faced whenever one desires to treat households, businesses or firms, nations, or any other conglomerate of individual persons. The question is really part of the general hypothesis that individuals maximize something, whether it be a utility function, a profit function, a probability of election function, or any other function or variable; indeed, a maximization hypothesis imposes restrictions on possible behavior patterns, all of which can be summarized by saying that the maximizing unit's ranking of alternatives must be consistent. This is a requirement which is tolerably easy to visualize for individuals, but more difficult for groups. In fact to deal with this problem at the level of countries and of groups, economists[1] often assume that all individuals making up the group have identical preference orderings *and* that each and every one consumes commodities in the same proportion, whatever their income.[2] In the present context, this way of treating the problem would lead one to suppose that all members of a given political party or coalition have identical orderings of policies and that the exact composition or mix of these policies would not change as the revenue of the government changed. This is a possible solution to the necessity of using groups as decision-making units and of insuring consistent orderings, but it is not an intuitively appealing, nor a theoretically very satisfactory, one and not one that will be adopted here.

Another solution to the problem of generating a consistent scale of preferences for groups and the one espoused in this study is to assume that there exists within the group a mechanism analogous to a market or exchange mechanism through which policies are traded and therefore valued or

1. See, for example, P. A. Samuelson, "Social Indifference Curves," *Quarterly Journal of Economics* (February 1956), pp. 1–22.
2. The assumption that utility functions are homothetic.

weighted and ranked in such a way as to reflect the preference ordering or scale of priorities of the group as a whole. Such a mechanism, through which individual utility functions such as (7.1) are in effect aggregated into a community or coalition utility function, presupposes the possibility of trading political support on one issue or policy for support on another; for example, it presupposes that when it is advantageous to do so, politician A consents to vote as B wishes on one decision in return for B's agreement to vote as he, A, wishes on another.

To visualize the operation of such a mechanism, assume that within the governing coalition or party, decisions are taken sequentially; to simplify the exposition, consider only decisions that have two outcomes which may be labeled 1 and 2 respectively. Assume now that the utility derived from outcome 1 of decision i by politician p is equal to U_{ip}^1 and the utility from outcome 2 of the same decision to be U_{ip}^2. Assume further that the importance which politician p attaches to decision i is given by the absolute difference between the utility he attaches to outcome 1 and 2 or by

$$r_{ip} = |U_{ip}^1 - U_{ip}^2| \qquad (7.2)$$

If the assumption is also made that p's subjective probability estimate of a favorable outcome on decision i, given the control that he has over that decision, is w_{is}, he will engage in trade and thus seek to move the system from status s to status s' where his control (or power) is greater, if and only if

$$r_{ip}w_{is'} + r_{kp}w_{ks'} > r_{ip}w_{is} + r_{kp}w_{ks} \qquad (7.3)$$

or, rearranging terms, if and only if

$$r_{ip}(w_{is'} - w_{is}) > r_{kp}(w_{ks} - w_{ks'}) \qquad (7.4)$$

where $i = 1, \ldots, k, \ldots I$ and $p = 1, \ldots, P$.

It should be clear from this discussion that changes in the status of the system are usually associated with changes in the probabilities as happens when p's power is increased or reduced. To see this, suppose that when s' obtains, p's control over decision k is less than when it is s that obtains, but that his power over decision i is larger; then if the increased power over decision i is exactly matched by a reduction in his power over k,

$$w_{is'} - w_{is} = w_{ks} - w_{ks'} \tag{7.5}$$

and exchange will take place only if

$$r_{ip} > r_{kp} \tag{7.6}$$

Exchange between two politicians who are members of the same party or of the same coalition will take place if conditions (7.4) or (7.5) and (7.6) hold for at least one other politician in the party or coalition.[3] Such trading, exchange, or logrolling would, when equilibrium was reached, reflect the intensity with which policies are desired by the group as a whole.[4] The question, then, is whether such a mechanism has an institutional counterpart. Before answering that question, it should be noted that the institutional context of such a mechanism (cabinets, caucuses, legislatures, committees, conventions, and informal groupings of various sorts) will vary, and possibly

3. The first modern version of the argument just discussed can be found in G. Tullock, "Problems of Majority Voting," *J.P.E.* (December 1959), pp. 571–79 and in Buchanan and G. Tullock, *The Calculus of Consent*, chapter 10. The argument in the text relies principally on J. S. Coleman, "Collective Decisions," *Sociological Inquiry* (Spring 1964) pp. 166–81; "Foundations for a Theory of Collective Decisions;" and "The Possibility of a Social Welfare Function," *American Economic Review* (December 1966), pp. 1105–22.

4. There are reasons to believe that if certain conditions are met—related to the life-expectancy of a party or coalition and therefore to the probability that agreements can be broken—a stable equilibrium will obtain. See Coleman's "Reply" to R. E. Parks, "The Possibility of a Social Welfare Function: Comment," *American Economic Review* (December 1967), pp. 1311–17.

substantially, from one political system to another. In particular, one expects the institutional rules of valuation and of exchange to be different for parties in a parliamentary system organized on the British model than in a congressional system organized on the American one or even a parliamentary system organized on the Canadian model; the difference between these and that in a communist party should be still greater. However, behind these veils the basic mechanism, if it exists, should still be observable.

To support the idea that a mechanism resembling the one briefly described above does in fact exist, I present two types of evidence.[5] The first rests on the fact that members of political parties do in fact disagree with each other but that as a rule they keep on talking and discussing and searching for some form of agreement with one another. This process becomes almost tangible when it breaks down with the resignation of one or sometimes a few party members; in terms of the preceding discussion, this means that the difference between the "bid" and the "ask" prices for one particular policy, and possibly for a set of these, is too great and therefore no trade between members can take place. The second type of evidence rests on certain external activities of members of political parties: some members, by making speeches (advertising) to groups outside the party itself and by engaging in exercises whose purpose can only be understood as efforts to alter the relative amount of resources or control over which they have command in the party, try to influence the terms of trade in negotiations within

5. I do, however, share Downs' view that the mechanism has no institutional counterpart for collective decisions involving large groups of individuals as in a country, a state or province, a city, or for that matter a small town. A. Downs, "In Defence of Majority Voting," *Journal of Political Economy* (April 1961) pp. 192–99. The reason for this is simply that the costs of organizing logrolling on that scale are prohibitive.

the party. Much of the discussions on party and cabinet soli-
darity can be seen as efforts to impose constraints on this type
of behavior so that the distribution of resources or power in the
party will not be too much out of line with what is deemed
desirable.

In the foregoing discussion of how political parties or coalitions arrive at collective decisions, I have not taken into account
the fact that strategic considerations of a game theoretic nature
will play a role. I will not here examine how these strategic
considerations will affect the characteristics of the collective
utility functions, but only indicate that the importance of
strategic considerations in shaping the behavior of the decision-
making unit will depend to a large extent on properties of the
institutional framework. If, for example, the number of elected
representatives in the governing party exceeds the number which
the decision-rule states is required for a decision, some members
of the governing party will find it advantageous in bargaining
with other members of the same party to hold out for a higher
price. It is for that reason that in parliamentary systems governing parties that have been elected with large majorities often
have to develop ways and means of disciplining those who do
not want to engage in intraparty trade. It is for this reason also
that in such circumstances, the caucus of the party tends to be
run in a strict and even authoritarian fashion by the leader of
the party. When the majority of the governing party is not
large, the temptation of members to engage in disruptive strategic behavior is greatly reduced and as a consequence the
caucus will meet much more informally. Similarly, the behavior
of the House Whip will depend on the possibilities that an
excess majority—that is, the difference between the number
required for a favorable decision in the house and the number
of elected members in the governing party—gives to some
members of the party.

The second problem raised by the hypothesis that political parties seek to maximize a collectivized version of (7.1) or (to repeat) a utility function defined for the probability of their reelection (or election) and other variables relates to the concept of maximization itself. The problem originates in the institutional framework that characterizes the public sector since the institutional rules are that political parties do not have to run for office on a continuous basis, but only at discrete points in time. If we were contrasting the behavior of firms in competitive markets for private goods with that of political parties, we could say that the former have to maximize on a continuous basis, while the latter only maximize on a discrete basis. The problem here is that discrete maximization is not really maximization at all, at least on a strict view of maximization, and as a consequence a way must be found of reconciling discreteness with the hypothesis adopted about the behavior of politicians and of political parties. In the remainder of this section, I will suggest a way of proceeding toward that reconciliation, while recognizing that the scope for research here is still broad.

One could, for example, hypothesize that political parties maximize on a continuous basis by assuming first that they are risk-averters—that is, that they are characterized by a given constant low index of risk-taking—and by assuming second that the weights placed on the preferences of citizens over the length of the election period lead to the implementation of policies which are more in accordance with these preferences at the end of the period than they are at the beginning. Another way of stating the same idea is to say that in the earlier part of the election period politicians value policy by using a rate of time discount that is lower than that used by citizens, because for them at that time the future is worth more than the present, since it is only in the future that they must seek reelection. As time passes, however, and as a new election day approaches, governing politicians will use a higher and higher rate of discount until toward the end of the election period they strive to use a rate that is equal to the one used by the relevant group of citizens as this is determined by the decision-rules in force.[6]

To clarify and extend the argument, let us assume that all the citizens in this relevant group use the same rate of time discount and that this rate is constant over the election period, that is, between t_1 and t_2. This rate is portrayed as $r_c(t)$ in figure 7.1. The $r_p(t)$ and $r_p'(t)$ curves depict the behavior over time of two possible streams of discount or time rates used by the politicians in deciding on which policies to implement. The difference between $r_c(t)$ and $r_p(t)$ or $r_p'(t)$ provides us with a measure of the extent to which politicians depart from the preference of the relevant group of citizens in making decisions. If a conceptualization such as this one is accepted, the hypothesis that governing politicians maximize a utility function such as $U_p = U_p(\pi, a_m)$ on a continuous basis, subject to the constraints to be examined, implies that they continuously select a rate of discount or a weight for the preferences of citizens so as to insure that they are reelected. The values of $r_p(t)$ that will achieve this result depend on the extent to which the relevant citizens *remember* that their preferences have not been satisfied. Let us represent this memory factor by ρ_t and assume that it varies between zero and one in such a way that when $\rho_t = 0$, the difference between $r_c(t)$ and $r_p(t)$ or $r_p'(t)$ is not remembered at all, while when $\rho_t = 1$, it is fully remembered. Therefore $(1 - \rho_t)$ indicates the extent of memory loss. At any point of time what is remembered is equal to

$$\rho_t[r_c(t) - r_p(t)] \qquad (0 \leq \rho_t \leq 1) \qquad (7.7)$$

and over the election period, the remembered disparity between r_c and r_p is equal to

6. I am indebted to David K. Sheppard of the University of Birmingham for the idea underlying the discussion of this paragraph.

$$h = \int_{t_1}^{t_2} \rho_t [r_c(t) - r_p(t)] dt \qquad (0 \leq \rho_t \leq 1) \qquad (7.8)$$

If we temporarily assume ρ_t to be given, continuous maximization of (7.1) will mean that politicians choose values of $r_p(t)$ such that h is made as small as possible. This way of formulating the problem implies that the decision-rules governing collective decisions are such that some of the a_m's can be set at positive levels and that it is still possible for politicians to be reelected. If the rules were such that the a_m's were always equal to zero, then for all $\rho_t > 0$ the $r_p(t)$ chosen by politicians would always be equal to $r_c(t)$.

Whether this approach salvages the concept of maximization as applied to (7.1), it provides part of an explanation or rationale for the often observed contour of the popularity ratings of governing parties as these are estimated by pollsters. These curves—a stylized version of which is depicted in the lower panel of figure 7.1—portray the proportion of the electorate declaring that it supports the governing party; they have been documented for a number of countries and for the United States for a number of years.[7] Using the arguments of the previous paragraphs and referring to the top panel of figure 7.1, there are two possible rationales for these curves. On the assumption that ρ_t—the memory factor—is equal to or in the neighborhood of zero, the contour of the popularity (or *P-*) curve could be said to reflect the difference between $r_c(t)$ and a stream such as $r_p'(t)$ since in that case everything in the past is remembered. On the other hand, if ρ_t is closer to one, the *P*-curve could be said to reflect the difference between the $r_c(t)$ and $r_p(t)$ curves, indicating that the recent past is more remembered than the distant past.

7. See, for example, V. O. Key, Jr., *The Responsible Electorate* (Cambridge: Harvard University Press, 1966).

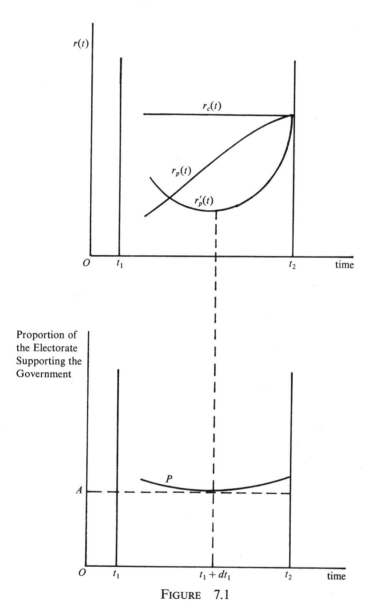

FIGURE 7.1

In concluding it should be mentioned that the minimum point on the P-curve—the one labeled $t_1 + dt_1$—need not always occur at the same phase of the election period. There is indeed some evidence that if $t_1 + dt_1$ appears too near to t_2 and/or if the support of the government falls too low (below a level such as A, for example), the support of the governing party may be permanently jeopardized for the elections at t_2.[8]

3. The Opposition

Analogies with duopoly and oligopoly theories, as these apply to certain markets for private goods, have often been used by economists to discuss competition between political parties in the public sector.[9] As Buchanan has already pointed out, these analogies carry us only part of the way, since once elected a political party is to some extent (but to some extent only) free from competition for the whole of the election period.[10] Furthermore, whatever the number of competitors, the fact that only one party can be in office at once (neglecting coalition governments) is of central importance in understanding the behavior of the opposition; this follows from the fact that many of the amenities of public life do not accrue to members of the opposition parties. This problem, of course, does not exist in American congressional-type systems, since in these systems the competition is between the executive and the legislative and

8. See note 7 above.
9. Often quoted are H. Hotelling, "Stability in Competition," *Economic Journal* (March 1929) pp. 41–57. The most significant contributions in recent years is, Downs, *An Economic Theory of Democracy*.
10. J. M. Buchanan, "Democracy and Duopoly: A Comparison of Analytical Models," *American Economic Review* (May 1968) pp. 322–31. Buchanan limits his remarks on that point to the welfare aspects of political competition.

thus between fully participating members of the public sector and as a consequence is much stronger in these systems. Indeed, the weakness of opposition parties in British parliamentary-type systems, accompanied by weak competition, appears to be one of the dominant characteristics of these systems and one which makes any writer cautious in discussing the role of potential competitors.

If one is reasonably careful, it is most enlightning, without rejecting the role of potential competitors, to analyze the behavior of political parties in terms of the theory of monopoly.[11] One of the main complicating factors here, however, arises from the fact that economists do not possess a substantively very relevant theory of monopoly in private markets, mostly, I suppose, because very few, if any, monopolies exist in the real world of private goods. If we think of monopoly as the absence of competition, it seems reasonable to assume that a monopolist is an entrepreneur able to depart from cost minimization and to disregard the preferences of consumers (at least in part) since there are no external forces—and even no internal ones, save the single-minded love of net money income, unencumbered by any other preoccupation and objective—to require him to do so, as there are when competition is strong and vigorous. Put another way, in the absence of competition—of necessity an external force—there are only weak reasons to believe that a monopolist would minimize costs and seek to satisfy the preferences of consumers and thus maximize profits. Similarly, in the absence of competition, a governing political party will not do everything it can to satisfy the preferences of citizens since weak competition implies a low probability of defeat and no com-

11. G. Tullock, "Entry Barriers in Politics," *American Economic Review* (May 1965) pp. 458–66.

petition means that the governing party does not have any replacement.[12]

One should not, however, push the analogy with monopoly too far since periodically governing parties have to run for re-election and potential competitors are usually real. The point of the preceding discussion was to emphasize that the tools that nongoverning parties can use in parliamentary-type systems are rather weak. They do not have the power to reduce taxes, to increase expenditures on policy S_1, while reducing it on S_2, etc. They can only criticize and make promises; activities that citizens rightly believe not to be very costly ones.

In the view adopted in this study, the main role of contending political parties in the determination of the level of public output is to provide criticism of those actions of the governing party that can profitably be criticized and to lead citizens to believe that if they were in office they would act in ways that are more in accordance with their preferences. Both these functions have the effect of raising ρ_t—the memory factor—and through this to force the governing party to satisfy the preferences of citizens more carefully and on a continuous basis. This view can be stated in a different fashion. The dominant characteristic of political competition—as distinguished from economic com-petition—is its asymmetry between competing parties. While in economic competition the tools or instruments that can be used by the competitors are largely the same, this is not the case in political competition since in this case the nongoverning parties and politicians cannot effectively alter the level and pattern of public policies.

One should also take note of the fact that even if parties and

12. On related problems, see M. Pinard, "One-Party Dominance and Third Parties."

politicians in the opposition have a very special role to play in the public sector, in that they are potential governing parties and politicians, other groups such as academics, social critics, and political writers as well as the press can also increase the level of competition to which the governing party is subjected. Indeed, in some societies at some times the competition that exists in the public sector comes not from the official opposition but from outside the public sector proper, from academics and others.

As is often the case, it is again instructive to look at communist regimes to understand the workings of democratic processes since these regimes try to reduce political competition to a minimum. Not only are opposition parties illegal and effectively banned, but the press is under the control of a state bureau, and other outside critics, analysts, and commentators are not permitted to express their views. Anyone venturing a public statement critical of the governing party is immediately classified as revisionist, antirevolutionary, and bourgeois. As economists have known for a long time, competition is never welcomed and is surely not something that a monopolist or a governing party would of itself foster.

In a non-trivial way, the main and dominant impact of the opposition is on the governing party itself and not on policies. For this reason if we label (c_t) the degree of internal and of external competition that originates with the contending parties and with the press, the academics, and the other social critics, we can rewrite equation (7.7) as:

$$\rho_t(c_t)[r_c(t) - r_p(t)] \qquad\qquad (0 \le \rho_t \le 1) \qquad (7.9)$$

and (7.8) as:

$$h^* = \int_{t_1}^{t_2} \rho_t(c_t)[r_c(t) - r_p(t)]dt \quad (0 \le \rho_t \le 1) \qquad (7.10)$$

and thus incorporate a large part of the effect of the role of the opposition in the model. In the following chapters, we will see how changes in c_t affect the level and composition of taxation and public expenditures.

8

Technical Constraints on the Behavior of the Governing Party

1. Introduction

The last chapter noted that a political party that maximizes a utility function defined for a probability of reelection and other variables could only do so subject to certain technical constraints or production conditions.[1] This chapter examines these constraints and analyzes how they define the range of feasible alternatives open to the governing party and how they influence its behavior and indirectly the supply of public output.

If the governing party is to maximize a function such as (7.1) $[U_p = U_p(\pi, a_m)]$, it will of necessity seek to enact and to implement policies that will satisfy the preferences of all those citizens whose support is required for its reelection, a number that is determined by the decision-rules governing the selection of the party that will govern. In the language of chapter 4, the governing party will seek to reduce and if possible to eliminate the coercion which some of its actions has or will impose on the

---

1. These constraints are additional to the physical constraints imposed by the production technology governing the combination of factors of production discussed in chapter 2.

members of the electorate that are decisive for its reelection.[2] To simplify the analysis of the problem facing the governing party, let us consider a jurisdiction of only two citizens, each characterized by a compensated technocratic demand curve for a single public policy and let us assume that the support of both is required if the governing party is to be reelected; let us further assume that the two citizens have equal incomes, but different tastes, and that the government pays for the public policy it implements by levying a proportional income tax which can be taken to represent the tax-price paid for the policy. The situation is portrayed in figure 8.1 where the A and B curves are the

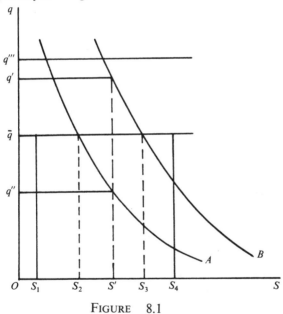

FIGURE   8.1

2.   I will not discuss the restrictions that prevent a majority from exploiting minorities until the end of this chapter, since this problem can be logically dissociated from the questions examined in this and the next four sections.

demand curves of the two citizens A and B, and $\bar{q}$ is the tax-price per unit of the policy S that is paid by each citizen.

Suppose that the *initial* decision of the government is to supply S_1 of S; we know from the discussion of part II as well as by observation of figure 8.1 that if the output is at such a level, both citizens will feel coerced and that if political participation costs are low, both will put pressure on the government to increase the quantity of S. Beginning at S_1, it is easy for the government to accommodate both citizens. As soon as S_2 is reached, however, any further increase in S will meet with the disapproval of A since beyond that point the marginal value of the income foregone to pay taxes, namely $\bar{q}$, will exceed his marginal valuation of S. B, on the other hand, will still put pressure on the government to increase S because for him the marginal value of S exceeds $\bar{q}$. As long as we are dealing with public policies which display characteristics of public goods (and of non-private goods), the governing party must face the fact that, over some ranges of supply, making A better off makes B worse off. Had the initial supply of S been S_4 instead of S_1, both individuals would have wanted a reduction in the level of the policy, but disagreement would have reappeared as soon as S_3 had been reached. We note that to the left of S_2 and to the right of S_3 the problem of obtaining the support of citizens is fundamentally trivial in that in these regions the supply of public policy is not subject to any special constraints; it is in the area between S_2 and S_3 that complications arise in that it is in this area that the particular constraints imposed by the technical characteristics of public goods are operative.

The same problem can profitably be illustrated in a different way. Suppose, again to simplify the exposition, that we are dealing with a jurisdiction with two citizens A and B and that the support of both is required if the government is to be re-elected. Imagine that to heat his house A uses bituminous coal which produces smoke and that *B* finds this smoke harmful to his health and to his general well-being. Now suppose that *A* and *B* do not speak the same language or that they come from different social classes so that the transaction costs of negotiations that would internalize that externality are so high that they are, in effect, prohibitive. Assume now that the government, for whatever reason, decides to require that *A* use non-bituminous coal or other types of fuels to produce the heat he wants. That decision elicits the support of *B* but meets with *A*'s disapproval since he must now pay more for the same amount of heat; had the government not taken the decision to regulate the behavior of *A*, *A* would have given his support to the governing party, while *B* would have withheld it.

The fact that the extent of coercion to which one citizen is subjected depends, in part, on the extent of coercion imposed on other citizens, is, from the point of view of the governing party, a technical constraint to which that party must respond and adjust. To do so it can engage in one or more of four basic activities; it can (1) enact and implement discriminatory policies as well as policies that have the characteristics of pure private goods, including changes in tax rates, basic exemptions, tax credits, loopholes, etc. (2) discriminatorily adjust the penalties levied against and the probability of apprehending those committing legal offenses; (3) engage in implicit logrolling, combined with full-line supply by combining policies in such a way as to elicit or maintain political support; and (4) seek to alter the preferences of citizens so as to reduce the differences that exist between them and thus make them more homogeneous.

In engaging in all of these activities, the governing party will seek to reduce the degree of coercion to which those citizens whose support it needs are subjected. The next sections will examine each of these activities, focusing on only one at a time and describing how each activity can lead to a reduction in the degree of coercion imposed on citizens. A final section examines the additional restrictions which a constitution imposes on the governing party.

2.   Discriminatory Policies and Private Goods[3]

A governing party seeking to maximize a utility function such as $U_p(\pi, am)$ will enact and implement certain discriminatory policies and supply a number of private goods in response to the technical constraints to which it is subjected. The same party will, however, also supply discriminatory policies and private goods because it is one of a number of methods by which it can insure that its own political organization will develop or at the very least not disintegrate. I have examined this second role of discriminatory policies at some length elsewhere and, since it is not directly related to the argument of this chapter, I will not repeat it here.[4]

To understand the first function played by discriminatory and private goods policies, one need only recognize that these policies are highly divisible and hence susceptible to differential adjustment between individuals. In other words, these policies, by their very nature, can be tailored to affect some individual or groups of individuals in a jurisdiction and not others. Such policies are illustrated by free school meals, by subsidized rents, by the construction of short spans of roads limited to one or

3.   Discrimination (and discriminatory policies) is a difficult word to use. If the tax-prices levied on all citizens are equal for each and every one of them, though the citizens have different preferences, then discrimination exists. On the other hand, if governments treat some individuals differently than others, no discrimination will exist if the implemented policies are marginally adjusted to individual preferences. In the discussion that follows, the context defines the sense in which I use the word.

4.   *Discriminatory Government Policies in Federal Countries* (Montreal: Canadian Trade Committee, 1967).

two electoral ridings, by special tariff reductions on the import of newsprint, by the swift granting to certain groups of special work permits for foreign domestic help, by the imposition of immigration restrictions on certain classes of workers that will protect special groups of domestic laborers, by tax rebates and the granting of loopholes as well as programs of regional investment grants, to name but a few of a class of policies that seems almost boundless.[5]

Since these goods are divisible, the governing party can distribute them in such a way as to reduce the degree of coercion felt by citizens. The discussion can be made more explicit by returning to figure 8.1. We have already seen that if the quantity of a policy supplied by the government falls between S_2 and S_3, any increase (or reduction) in the amount of S will make one citizen worse off or, put another way, will increase the extent of coertion imposed on him. To be specific, let us suppose that the government provides S' of S so that both A and B are initially coerced. Increasing the supply of S toward S_3 will improve B's situation, but worsen A's, while a reduction toward S_2 will worsen B's situation, and improve A's. If the governing party decides to maintain S' of S, it could at the same time give a subsidy (in money or in kind) to A and levy an extra tax on B in such a way that for both citizens the marginal value of the public policy (S) is equal to its tax-price ($\bar{q}$) corrected for the subsidy and for the tax. Citizen B would not, of course, be as well-off as he was before the excess tax since the amount of free benefits he is now receiving is zero, but as long as the marginal value he places on S is at least as large as the marginal value of his private outlays, he will by the argument and assumption of chapter 4 still support the governing party. The subsidy that will be paid to A at a rate of q'' will be equal to the excess tax

5. I have given a large number of examples in *Discriminatory Government Policies*, chapters 1–4.

levied on B at a rate of q', and hence the government could not pay the subsidy without levying the excess tax.[6] The governing party could alternatively and with the same consequences increase the tax-price levied on both citizens from $\bar{q}$ to q''' and give to each citizen an unequal subsidy (again in money or in kind) that would equalize the respective tax rates with the relevant marginal values of S.

It must be emphasized that given the supply of public output S', it may not be possible for the governing party to levy an excess tax of amount $(q'-\bar{q})$ equal to $(q-\bar{q}'')$ that will elicit the support of both A and B. This follows from the fact that the size of the excess tax and that of the subsidy depend on the elasticity of the demand curves, and, of course, there is no need for these elasticities to be in a relationship to one another so that the governing party's budget will be balanced. In a situation of this kind, the governing party must, in addition to deciding on the level of q' and q'', alter the level of S. By changing these three variables, it can always eliminate coercion on both A and B and balance its budget.

The foregoing analysis implicitly assumes that taxes and subsidies could either be paid in money or in kind and that one form of payment was equivalent to the other. Since I have neglected the cost of operating the government itself, I have, in effect, assumed that $1.00 received by A costs $1.00 to B whether it is paid in money or in kind. This is surely not the case. The costs of paying subsidies in kind must be much higher than paying them in money (similarly for taxes, though, except for such policies as conscription, these are less often levied in kind).

6. I am for the moment disregarding the situation that would arise if the governing party chose to levy the excess-tax (the difference between q' and q) on citizens that are not in the group of those that have to support the governing party if it is to be reelected. This question is discussed in section 6 below.

While I do not wish to suggest an hypothesis to explain the observed preference for subsidies in kind until the next chapter, it is worth noting, for the argument of the present chapter, that this preference implies that to finance a $1.00 subsidy to *A*, the government will have to collect more than $1.00 in excess taxes from *B*.

Furthermore, if citizens have a preference for subsidies in money, subsidies in kind that are larger will have to be given them to maintain their support. If, for example, a subsidy of $1.00 paid in money was equal to $(\bar{q}-q'')$ in figure 8.1 and thus would be sufficient to elicit the support of *A*, a subsidy in kind would have to be larger than $1.00 unless *A* was indifferent as between $1.00 in money and $1.00 in kind or had a preference for subsidies in kind.

Paying subsidies in kind, therefore, will usually entail excess costs on the supply side of the public sector as well as on the demand side and as a consequence the preceeding discussion relating to figure 8.1 must be altered to include these excess costs. The alteration is straightforward, however, since the excess costs can be added to the taxes levied and to the subsidies paid out at least as long as the cost of producing public output can be assumed to be constant and as long as the marginal rate of substitution between *S* and the subsidies in kind can be supposed to be zero for the citizens receiving them.

It is of some interest to note that subsidies in kind tend to be fairly closely related to the income position of the recipients. If we assume that such subsidies as school meals, milk and orange juice programs, food stamps, subsidized rents, medicare and medicaid policies are the type provided to lower income groups when these are thought to be the ones that are coerced by the implementation of some public policies, while subsidies to the arts, to painting and sculpture, to museums, to the cinema, to the theater, to high-brow broadcasting, to air travel, to owner-occupied houses, and to higher education are paid to higher income groups when these are deemed to be the ones that are coerced by the enactment of certain policies,[7] then one would tend to observe that ceteris paribus,[8] the expenditure pattern of jurisdictions with steeply progressive tax structures (and therefore of jurisdictions most likely to induce coercion in higher income groups) would also be the ones subsidizing programs that are mostly consumed by higher income groups.

In their classic study, Peacock and Wiseman documented for the United Kingdom the tendency toward centralization of functions that had historically been performed by local governments, a tendency, which for the period they cover, is also observable for other countries such as Canada and the United States.[9] This phenomenon is capable of partial explanation within the framework presented here since in all these cases the volume of pure or quasipure public goods provided by the senior government of these countries was increasing, sometimes sharply, and as a consequence it was felt necessary to increase the provision of private goods—goods whose supply was, in all cases, constitutionally allocated to the junior governments—in order to reduce and, if possible, eliminate the degree of coercion induced by the former.

---

7. It may be well to recall here that not all subsidies need be discriminatory subsidies; to put it differently, subsidized broadcasting, subsidized music, etc., need not be bribes-in-kind given to some groups to compensate them for coercion originating elsewhere; they could be the original policy objectives of governments, not the ones used as bribes. Whether they are, or not, is strictly an empirical problem, albeit a difficult one.

8. A ceteris paribus related to the level and structure of political participation costs and to that of bargaining between politicians and bureaucrats. (See chapter 10.)

9. A. T. Peacock and J. Wiseman, *The Growth of Public Expenditure in the United Kingdom*.

3. The Discriminatory Enforcement of Laws

A governing party (government) is not interested in law enforcement per se, that is, it is not interested in the discovery, apprehension, conviction, and punishment of criminals, offenders, or lawbreakers as such.[10] It is only because, to maximize $U_p = U_p(\pi, am)$, it has to eliminate or at least to curtail the damage and the harm which the actions of some citizens impose or could impose on others that a governing party enacts laws and then enforces and polices them.[11]

In the execution of that task, the governing party has control over the following variables: (1) the type of laws enacted; (2) the probability of apprehending and of convicting those who violate these laws; and (3) the penalties—fines and prison terms—that are imposed on those who are apprehended and convicted. In the discussion that follows, I assume that optimal laws, somehow defined, are always enacted and that the only problem facing the governing party consists in deciding on (2) and (3). This is not a very restrictive assumption since a good

10. In an important article on "Crime and Punishment: An Economic Approach," *Journal of Political Economy* (March–April 1968), pp. 169–217, Gary S. Becker presents an analysis of law enforcement that has influenced the present analysis in a number of ways, though his analysis is aggregative and normative in that his results depend on the minimization of a social loss function or, in more traditional language, on the maximization of a social welfare function; furthermore, the rationale he postulates for illegal activities is different from the one assumed here. The two approaches however, have a number of points in common. For a still different approach, but one that is also normative, see S. Rottenberg, "The Clandestine Distribution of Heroin, Its Discovery and Suppression," *Journal of Political Economy*. See also, G. J. Stigler, "The Enforcement of Laws" (Mimeo, 1969).

11. The argument will be formally developed in terms of damages; it can, however, be extended to the case of laws which do not elminate or reduce damages, but instead generate benefits directly.

law (defined in terms of its contribution to the governing party's utility) badly enforced can be defined as a bad law. If it seems as a restrictive assumption, the following discussion should make clear how it could be modified.

Throughout, I will assume that the level of law enforcement, that is, the level of the probability of apprehending lawbreakers and the level of punishments meted out to those who are apprehended and convicted, is set by the governing party. It is, of course, true that in practice the courts, and not the governing party, determine the exact penalty to be levied on apprehended offenders, but it is also true that governments set *the range* over which the courts have freedom to act. In the remainder of this section, I will therefore neglect the complications that arise from the indeterminacy in the size of punishments resulting from the freedom granted to the courts. Furthermore, I will assume that the probability of apprehending violators is under the control of the governing party even if in practice this control is located in a police bureau.[12]

To understand the problems that are peculiar to law enforcement, we must examine the nature and the extent of the damages that result when laws are not enacted or when they are violated. Some damages, though external to the individual perpetrating the offense, are external to such a limited extent that the harm or damage imposed on others is virtually nil and as a result these damages are really private; this is the case when an individual chooses to worship God in his own home even though the law explicitly forbids him to do so or when two consenting adults engage in homosexual activity in the privacy of their house again against the explicit dictates of the law.

---

12. That bureau will behave like all other bureaus and as a consequence that analysis of the determinants of law enforcement will only be completed when the analysis of the behavior of bureaus and that of their interaction with politicians has been concluded in the next three chapters.

Other damages are more external or public as when individuals engage in tax avoidance, in burglaries, in other felonies, or in the distribution of narcotics; and finally, some damages are almost completely public as when individuals drive their cars recklessly or pollute the environment.[13] To put it in a different way, the violation of laws generates damages which run the full spectrum from being almost private to being almost completely public.

It is noteworthy that the damages from lawbreaking need not be real or physical in any objective sense; it is sufficient that the damages be felt for them to have the effects described below. For example, the objective damages from violating a censorship law by importing a banned book or film are really zero for those who do not read the book or see the film, but some of these persons may still feel offended by the knowledge that such activities are going on and, for the purpose of the present analysis, that is all that is required.

In the application of the analysis that follows, it may sometimes be useful to distinguish between symmetric and asymmetric damages. The first of these exists when both of two citizens A and B can engage in a given activity and thereby impose damages on each other. Most legal offenses are of this kind. To see this, one must not think of a world in which some citizens are lawabiding, while others are not, but of a world before the enactment of any given law where the a priori probability that an individual will engage in a given activity must be assumed to be the same as that for every other individual. The second type of damages—the one labeled asymmetric—arises when an action of A imposes damages on B, while B cannot himself engage in that activity and hence cannot

13. Tax avoidance has external effects since with a given level of expenditures, avoidance by one individual implies that others will have to pay more.

harm A. Such a situation would arise, for example, if, given the prevailing winds, the smoke from A's stacks in New Jersey harmed B who lives in Massachusetts, while the smoke from B's chimney seldom, if ever, reached A. This type of damage may not be very common, but it certainly exists.

To proceed with the analysis, it is not essential to make the distinction between the two types of damages continuously; we can therefore assume that A and B—two citizens whose support is needed by the governing party if it is to be reelected—both derive positive benefits from a law which prohibits a certain activity because this prohibition reduces or even eliminates the symmetric damages which this activity generates.[14] It remains true, however, that each one of the two citizens would find it advantageous to break the law as long as the other one did not do so, hence the necessity of law enforcement. But law enforcement is costly and, as a result, we must inquire what constitutes the best level of law enforcement. To put it differently, we must ask how much law enforcement a governing party seeking to maximize equation (7.1) will provide.

To answer this question, I take it that the probability of apprehending lawbreakers is positively related to the amount of resources allocated to that activity. In other words, I assume that the chances of apprehending a violator will increase ceteris paribus (a ceteris paribus almost exclusively related to the total number of violations at a point of time) with increases in the number of policemen, patrol cars, and other equipment in the hands of the police bureau. Increasing the probability of ap-

14.   This statement does not in any way imply that the only way of eliminating external damages is through public legislation, nor does it imply that all policing is or should be public. Indeed, it may be that the bulk of policing is provided privately, but I am not concerned with the analysis of this activity in the present chapter. (For an analysis that deals with self-provision see chapter 5.)

prehending violators by allocating resources to that activity will imply either an increase in taxation or a reduction in the supply of this and/or other government polices or both. For analytical convenience I assume that law enforcement is financed by taxation and ask how much of it will be desired by A and B.

A (and B) will wish to see a level of law enforcement so that the marginal tax cost to him of deterring $B(A)$ from engaging in the activity that generates net external marginal damages[15] and which is prohibited by law will not exceed the value of the marginal damages imposed by the activity if $B(A)$ engages in it, while $B(A)$ will be deterred from engaging in the activity if the marginal expected costs [the probability of apprehension (p) times the marginal value of the punishment (Δf)] exceed the marginal benefits from engaging in the activity.[16] There is no reason to believe that the level of law enforcement desired by A and B should be equal, any more than there is to believe that A and B would be equally deterred from engaging in the illegal activity at any given level of marginal expected costs.

Given this assumption, given the net damages which are imposed on A if B engages in X, and given the relationship between expenses and the degree of law enforcement, we immediately know the maximum tax-price that can be levied on A to finance law enforcement if A is going to support the governing party; since B's allegiance to the governing party will be

---

15.   The damages are net damages, that is, gross damages netted for insurance benefits and corrected for the costs of insurance.

16.   To extend this argument to a world where there are more than two individuals, one must make an assumption about the distribution of the costs of law enforcement and changes therein among the various citizens of the jurisdiction. The problem is in every way similar to the one encountered in chapter 4 relating to the distribution of tax burdens between public policies and citizens. The aggregative model of chapter 4 is not extended to the discussion of the present section.

determined by similar considerations, we must conclude that the value of damages from breaking the law determines the maximum values of both p and f and since the valuation of damages will usually differ between A and B, p and f will have to discriminatorily adjust to their respective valuations if the governing party is going to be reelected. Given the fact that both p and f are highly divisible, that goal is an achievable one.

The foregoing argument implies that if damages from law-breaking are small, both p and f will be low for both citizens, though they will not necessarily be the same and the incidence of offences will be high. It further implies that if A places a high value on damages, while B does not, p_B and f_B will be set at a high level so as to deter offenses, while p_A and f_A will be at a low level.

The preceding discussion has been developed in terms of punishments (f) without distinguishing between fines and prison sentences. In deciding between these two forms of punishment, the governing party will take the following factors into account: (1) the income and welfare of the offender and (2) the net cost of imprisonment that the innocent must pay. If offenders are poor, they will be imprisoned unless the net costs of imprisonment are so high that the innocents are not willing to meet them either because they are themselves poor or simply because they are unwilling to meet them and then the governing party will have to resort to capital punishment.[17] These costs can be high if the external gross damages are high and the length of the sentence thus necessarily long and, at the same time, if the offenders are the dregs of society. If, however, offenders can be rehabilitated through the use of modern psychiatry and therapy

17. One implication of this analysis is that the incidence of capial punishment is not necessarily related to the extent of the damages resulting from violating laws unless these affect the cost of imprisonment but they are related (1) to the income and wealth position of offenders; (2) the costs of imprisonment; and (3) to the willingness of the law abiders to meet these costs.

as well as other methods of training or retraining, they can be put on parole and with the growth of modern computers their whereabouts can be easily checked so that they can be made to earn an income higher than the one they would have earned before retraining; furthermore, given the introduction of generalized systems of progressive income taxation they can be taxed in such a way as to reduce the long-run costs of imprisonment to the innocents. The decision about levying a fine or imposing a prison sentence will then be largely determined by comparing the net revenues from fines with the net revenues from taxing the income stream of the capital invested in rehabilitation skills and the training of prisoners.

4.   Implicit Logrolling and Full-Line Supply

The term *implicit logrolling* refers to the action of trading policies one against another as distinguished from the trading of votes which is the prime concern of explicit logrolling or logrolling proper.[18] To put it differently, logrolling proper takes the set of possible policies (or the platform of political parties) as given and describes the exchange of votes (with or without monetary side payments) that produces the best set of policies, while implicit logrolling takes the possible patterns of voting as given and describes the rearrangement of policies that will also be best in some sense. This activity is, therefore, closely related to what I have earlier called "full-line supply."

Implicit logrolling combined with full-line supply can be used by a governing party as a device to remain in office, while not satisfying all the demands of those whose support it needs to be reelected. To understand this proposition, suppose that a

18.   The term is from Buchanan and Tullock, *The Calculus of Consent*, though they define it in a different way than I do.

citizen dislikes a given policy—call it S_1—which the governing party wants to implement for reasons which need not concern us here, but assume that his dislike is small, though sufficient, taken by itself, to induce him to withhold his support from the governing party and transfer it to an opposition party. If, however, that citizen has a strong positive preference for S_2 and if the governing party decides to introduce that policy in the overall bundle of policies it will implement, while the opposition party (or parties) does not, the citizen will still vote for the governing party for the sake of obtaining S_2, though he mildly dislikes S_1 which will also be implemented.

Implicit logrolling could be used to satisfy the constrained demands of citizens, but in the hands of a political party and combined with full-line supply, it will be used to counterbalance the negative impact that one policy has on the political adherence of some citizens through the implementation of some unrelated policy. As the foregoing discussion indicates, the freedom of the governing party to engage in that activity depends on the behavior and aggresiveness of the opposition party or parties; if the opposition had countered by promising to implement S_2 as the governing party did and if the citizen had believed the promise, the governing party would have lost the support of that citizen.[19]

It is of interest to note, as a conclusion, that the obverse of implicit logrolling is the formation of Downs' coalitions of minorities.[20] These appear whenever an opposition party can appeal to minority groups by including in its platform those

19.   In addition, since the extent of full-line supply depends on the distribution of functions between levels of government in a federation (as well as on the number of levels and of governments), the extent to which a governing party can elicit the support of citizens without satisfying all their preferences also depends on that distribution (see chapter 3 above).

20.   A. Downs, *An Economic Theory of Democracy*, chapter 4.

policies for which they have a strong preference, but which the governing party cannot, for one reason or another, implement. By appealing in this way to a large enough number of minorities, it is able to form a majority and to capture the apparatus of state.

5. Search and Advertising

The analysis of the last three sections should have made clear that the constraints on the behavior of the governing party are largely related to the differences that exist in the preferences (and incomes) of the citizens whose support is needed if the governing party is to be reelected. If tastes were similar, the problems of government would be greatly simplified. Accordingly, the governing party will allocate considerable money, time, and effort to advertising, that is, to an activity designed (or so the government hopes) to alter the preferences of citizens in such a way as to make them more homogeneous.

The advertising efforts of governing parties will often be made easier by the efforts of some citizens to try to influence the preferences of others. Indeed, in many instances efforts to alter the tastes of some citizens may be initiated by a group of citizens who will then receive the support of the governing party. Note that when the governing party supports one group of citizens in its efforts to influence another, that this will simplify its task, but that the resulting supply of public output is likely to be different than what would obtain if the government was using advertising to influence all citizens in like fashion.

Search—surveys, polls, grass-root canvassings, consultations, maintaining contacts, releasing trial balloons, and a host of other devices—is designed to provide the governing party with information about the intensity with which preferences are held but more importantly about the differences in tastes that exist in the electorate. One should note that even though advertising can be conducted without prior knowledge of the preferences of citizens, such a knowledge is useful in that it can increase its efficiency. For that reason search and advertising will be closely related. Since both are costly they will be engaged in to the point where their marginal cost to the governing party is no larger than marginal value, both magnitudes measured in terms of the objective function U_p [$= U_p (\pi, am)$].[21]

We have very little knowledge of political advertising—though more is known of the extreme form of political advertising called propaganda—and of its quantitative importance in the political process as compared with substitutes such as the implementation of discriminatory and private good policies, the use of discriminatory law enforcement, and the utilization of implicit logrolling.[22] Part of the explanation for this state of affairs rests in the malaise that most analysts experience in saying that the activity of a governing party aimed at ascertaining, changing, and standardizing the preferences of the electorate is advertising. However that may be, it should be noted, in conclusion, that the money costs—though not necessarily the time and energy costs—of political advertising are fairly low and, therefore, that there is a large amount of it.[23] Also, government advertising is not regulated and, as a result, the amount

21. See G. J. Stigler, "The Economics of Information," *Journal of Political Economy* (June 1961), pp. 213–25.

22. Much of what is known about propaganda as well as advertising is well summarized in V. O. Key, Jr., *Politics, Parties and Pressure Groups* (New York: Thomas Y. Crowell, 1944); see also S. Tchakhotine, *Le Viol des Foules* (Paris: Gallimard, 1952).

23. Daily newspapers, for example, by reporting and often commenting on the speeches, declarations, exhortations, and justifications of politicians, often devote as much if not more space to the efforts of these officials to change and mold the preferences of the electorate and hence the demand for government policies, than they allocate to the efforts of businesses to change the demand for their product.

of it which is misleading and deceptive tends to be a fairly large proportion of the total.

6. The Constitution

This is not the place to develop a theory of the role that constitutions play in the political process, but it is essential that we take note of one of these roles. The discussion of the previous sections focused exclusively on the citizens who, given the decision-rules governing the choice of the governing party, must support the government if this latter is to be reelected and assumed that all the adjustments were limited to these citizens. In other words, I assumed throughout that the governing party, though it would find it profitable to do so, did not discriminate against minorities. It did not, for example, levy a tax on members of the minority to finance a subsidy to members of the majority so as to reduce the degree of coercion to which these latter were subjected. It did not either charge larger fines to members of the minority so as to be able to reduce the costs of law enforcement for the majority.

Governing parties do not care for minorities, and though the uncertainty that exists about who constitutes the majority will prevent them from exploiting minorities, they will be stopped principally by the (written or unwritten) constitution. To put it differently, those citizens whose support is *not* needed for the governing party's reelection will be protected from exploitation, to the extent that they are, by the constitution. Constitutions come in all manners and forms and the interpretation given them varies a great deal so that governments will be able to reduce the coercion to which some members of the majority are subjected by exploiting the minority, but the extent of their freedom to do so will depend on the degree to which the constitution is explicit in defining the rights of individual citizens, on the interpretation given these clauses by the courts, but principally by the highest courts, and on the cost of suing the government if it is judged to have breached the articles of the constitution. The more precise the constitution in defining the rights of citizens, the more extensive these rights; the more constructionist the courts and the lower the costs of initiating legal procedures, the less will the governing party be able to exploit the minority to gain the support of the majority.

7. The Selected Alternative

The foregoing sections have discussed each alternative open to the governing party separately. Nowhere have I indicated which one, or which ones, of the alternatives would be chosen. The reason for this is simple. To choose between the available alternatives, the governing party has to be provided with relative costs. It is not until chapter 10 that these costs will be introduced and defined and hence it is not until that chapter that the choice problem will be resolved.

9

The Behavior of Bureaus

1. The Hypothesis

Decisions about the supply of public policies are made by politicians, but these decisions are influenced and sometimes largely shaped by bureaucrats. It is therefore not possible to analyze the forces that impinge on the provision of public output without including bureaus and bureaucrats in the framework of analysis.

Consequently, in the following discussion and in the remainder of this study, I assume that bureaucrats maximize a utility function defined for one variable only, that is, for the relative size of their bureaus.[1] Since I also assume that the total utility of bureaucrats increases as this variable increases, this hypothesis is equivalent to one which states that bureaucrats seek to maximize the relative size of their bureaus. To proceed with the analysis, I define the size of bureaus by the number of in-

---

1. W. A. Niskanen assumed that bureaus maximize the absolute size of their budgets; see his *Bureaucracy and Representative Government*, (Chicago: Aldine-Atherton, 1971), pp. 38 and ff. 80. The hypothesis adopted here, though modified, is taken from Niskanen; I do not, however, follow him beyond the adoption of his suggested objective function.

dividuals in the bureau; in the application of the hypothesis, it may in some cases be more useful to define the size of the bureau in terms of the money expenditures of the bureau and in this case the hypothesis would say that bureaucrats seek to maximize the budget of their bureau relative to the government's total budget.

The hypothesis implies, even when stated in its simplified form (bureaucrats seek to maximize the relative size of their bureaus), that it is through the maximization of this objective that bureaucrats are able to achieve the highest possible income and prestige consistent with the constraints to which they are subjected and which I will examine below.[2] It also implies that bureaucrats are not responsive to the preferences of citizens, but are solely guided in their actions by the network of relationships linking them to politicians and to other bureaucrats and bureaus. The fact that the behavior of bureaucrats is to some extent determined by interaction with politicians implies, of course, some indirect response to the preferences of citizens, since politicians are, given the institutional framework, responsive to these preferences; but except for this relationship bureaucrats have a professional life of their own and a pattern of behavior unrelated to the preferences of citizens.

In the practical application of the hypothesis, one should be careful to take note that in some systems, such as the American political system, the political life of some bureaucrats is closely related to the political life of politicians and that, as a result, these bureaucrats will tend to be as responsive to the preferences of citizens as the politicians are. In applying the hypothesis in

---

2.   The addition of prestige to income serves only to emphasize that these two variables are closely related. Should it turn out that they were not, one would have to drop the mention of prestige and not that of income since the discussion of the production conditions in the next section of this chapter applies to income.

such systems, it would probably be better to assimilate these bureaucrats with the politicians and to apply the bureaucracy-hypothesis to individuals at lower levels in the bureaus.

Finally, the hypothesis implies that bureaucrats have preferences of their own regarding public policies and public output and that they will seek to satisfy these preferences. This will lead them to adopt typically bureaucratic behaviors; for example, bureaucrats will emphasize the benefits and under-estimate costs in cost-benefit studies;[3] they will favor a rate of discount in estimating the present value of benefits and costs which will make large projects look more profitable than they really are;[4] they will support the introduction of complicated and elaborate machinery to deal with the problem of rising prices and money incomes and other issues; they will systematically redefine the objectives and the purpose of a program to insure that it remains up-to-date;[5] they will favor the introduction of new legislation to correct the ill effects of some older policy, instead of recommending the abolition of the old policy; they will give support to programs that require or are made to require transfers in kind instead of transfers in money, since the former have a higher labor requirement per unit of value transferred than the latter; they will generally favour economic planning and a host of other similar activities.

3. Interestingly enough, it appears that bureaus seldom if ever err in the direction of overestimating the costs of projects and programs, but underestimate them—and by amounts that usually exceed some unforeseen rate of price increase.

4. One way of doing this is to use the same rate of discount for all projects, whatever the uncertainty that attaches to the various estimates of cost and benefit, as is done in the United Kingdom. See F. Juhasz, *An Analytical Study of the Economics of Water Barrage Schemes and Public Goods* (unpublished Ph. D. diss, University of London, 1969).

5. For the case of the housing legislation in the United Kingdom, see F. G. Pennance and H. Gray, *Choice in Housing* (London: Institute of Economic Affairs, 1968).

2. The Technical Constraints

Bureaucrats maximize the relative size of their bureaus subject to some technical constraints which define the range of feasible alternative behaviors between which they can choose. These constraints exist for all bureaus, large or small, powerful or weak, private or public; but as with other technical constraints they are subject to change. In the following discussion, I will not be concerned with the analysis of the factors which can lead to changes in the technical constraints and hence the discussion will be mostly static; at various points, however, I will take note of mechanisms which underlie some adjustment processes in the "production" conditions constraining the behavior of bureaucrats.

To maximize the relative size of their bureaus, bureaucrats will withhold and/or transform information as it moves from lower to higher echelons in the hierarchical structure of their bureau and/or they will withhold or transform commands as they move in the opposite direction, in such a way that bureaucrats placed "higher-up" in the hierarchical structure and the politicians will develop a "good" image of "lower" bureaucrats and accede to their demands. This phenomenon—which is reinforced by the "natural" force of entropy (see below)—applies to single bureaus as well as to structures of bureaus; it has been called "control-loss" by Tullock.[6] To summarize, control-loss arises when bureaucrats receiving information from a lower hierarchical level distort that information when passing it to their superiors because by so doing they can maxi-

6. Tullock, *The Politics of Bureaucracy*. A. Downs has pushed that analysis further: *Bureaucratic Structure and Decision-Making* (Santa Monica, Calif.: The Rand Corporation, Memorandum RM–4646–1–PR, October 1966), and *Inside Bureaucracy* (Boston: Little, Brown, 1967), which largely duplicates *Bureaucratic Structure and Decision-Making*.

mize the relative size of their budget or their share in their bureau's budget and hence their personal incomes and status. In more general terms, one can say that officials at a given hierarchical level will discover that by altering the messages received (and to be transmitted) even slightly—that is, by withholding all or part of the information that is detrimental to them and forwarding only what their superiors would most like to learn—they can achieve their objectives. Since officials at all hierarchical levels in the organization must be assumed to be doing the same thing, the information that finally reaches the ultimate decision-makers would normally be incomplete, biased, and unreliable. Control-loss is thus the natural result of the facts that budgets are approved by higher bureaus and by politicians that are higher in the hierarchical structure and that the income and prestige of bureaucrats in all bureaus depend on the relative size of bureaus.

The total loss or leakage (L) of information and/or commands to higher echelons in a bureau and to bureaus placed higher up in the organizational structure and to politicians is equal to

$$L = (1 - a_1)^{n-1} \qquad (9.1)$$

where a_1 is the share or proportion of a message that is transmitted and n is the number of hierarchical levels in a bureau or in an organization.

Control-loss arising with what I have previously called the natural force of entropy is something which—unlike the behavioral control-loss just described—is largely outside the designs of the members of the bureaucracy. As sometimes represented that kind of control-loss seems to have an inexorable character about it; it is seen as a force that cannot readily be controlled and that would certainly not respond to changes in relative rewards and in relative costs. Most of the corroborative evidence on this type of control-loss—and there is a large amount of it—comes from experiments that have been designed to ascertain its existence and to measure its strength in the mechanical transmission of signals, sounds, written words and pictures, and a score of other similar signals; it has never been measured in bureaucratic organizations. If we add the natural to the behavioral control-loss, (9.1) becomes

$$L = [1 - (a_1 + a_2)]^{n-1} \qquad (9.2)$$

where $(1 - a_2)$ measures the proportion of a message that is lost through entropy.

Decision-makers in any organization are, of course, aware that leakages, like the ones described, are occurring—maybe because a number of them have at one time or another been bureaucrats themselves—and since they are maximizing an objective function of their own they will undertake to reduce, to the extent possible, the role of this barrier to the attainment of their own ultimate objective .There are basically two types of things that they can do. First, they can introduce anti-distortion devices in the bureaucracy. These include among other things the creation of redundant bureaus, the introduction of overlapping zones of responsibility between bureaus, the re-organization of the bureaucratic structure to keep it flat (with small numbers of hierarchical levels), and external data checks taking the form of direct contacts with members at lower levels in the hierarchy over the heads of the higher level ones and also direct contacts with citizens and customers generally.[7] The use of these devices aimed at reducing control-loss is costly in money and in time and consequently the devices will only be used up to the point where their marginal contribution to the decision-makers' objective is at least as large as their marginal cost measured in the same terms.

7. These anti-distortion devices have been described and analyzed in detail by Downs, *Bureaucratic Structure and Decision-Making*, chapter 4.

The second thing that decision-makers can do to combat control-loss is to bribe their subordinates for part or for all of the information or messages which they have withheld. In the absence of strategic behavior on the part of decision-makers and bureaucrats, superiors will buy information from their subordinates up to the point where the marginal yield of information measured by its contribution to their own objective is just equal to the marginal costs to them measured in the same way.

The implicit and informal process of bargaining which this bribing and buying entails is crucially dependent on the absence of strategic behavior.[8] Before we look at the variable, it is well to note that, given the size of control spans (hierarchical levels), the larger the number of levels in an organization, the greater also the mass of information held by officials as we move up the hierarchical ladder and consequently the greater the sum of money or of other emoluments that decision-makers will have to pay in order to obtain the desired information. It follows that the total costs to politicians of acquiring undistorted information increases as the size of bureaucracy increases and that the salary structures in organizations will have the pyramidal shape so often observed.[9]

Still disregarding strategic behavior, we conclude that as the size of bureaus increases, a point is reached where the increasing costs of bribes and of anti-distortion devices to combat control-loss overtake the falling costs from economies of specialization that characterize organizations and thus deter-

8.   The extensive pattern of formal rules and informal structures so well documented by sociologists (see, for example, P. Selznick, "Foundations of the Theory of Organization," *American Sociological Review*, (February, 1948) pp. 26–30 and summarized by Downs (see note 7 above, pp. 47–68), which characterizes bureaucracies, certainly provides all the required ingredients for an active process of bargaining within the structure.

9.   See H. A. Simon, "The Compensation of Executives," *Sociometry* (March 1957), pp. 32–35.

mine the optimum size of organizational structures. Expansion beyond that size entails an unwarranted departure from the objective of decision-makers.[10]

Let us now focus on strategic behavior and note that the formal and informal structures so characteristic of bureaucracies have the resemblance they have because they are aimed at reducing the potential strategic behavior of decision-makers and of bureaucrats in the process of bargaining over the payments for information and these structures are largely successful in that endeavor. To put it in a different fashion, the system of rules, of checks and counterchecks, of informal contacts, of personal relationships, and of loyalties that have been described at length by students of organizations exist to minimize the role of strategic behavior in bureaus so that bargaining between superiors and subordinates can be carried out in the absence of bilateral conjectural variations. This point becomes more obvious once it is realized that most of these formal and informal rules are devised to induce each member of the organization to adopt a specific role which he will play as long as he occupies a given place in the organization. The surprise that is sometimes shown at the apparently complete transformation of someone as he leaves a job to undertake a new and different assignment is evidence of this phenomenon.

For these reasons, in the analysis of bureaucracies, it is usually possible to neglect strategic behavior without any significant analytical loss. Should strategic behavior within the organization turn out to be an important component in the adjustment processes characteristic of bureaus, it would have to be taken

---

10. Though based on different equilibrating mechanisms, the argument of this paragraph was inspired by O. E. Williamson's "Hierarchical Control and Optimum Firm Size," *Journal of Political Economy* (April 1967) pp. 123–38.

into account and its impact on the supply of public policies would have to be assessed. In the remainder of this study, I will assume that it does not exist.

3.   Some Empirical Regularities[11]

Following Wildavsky's painstaking descriptive analysis of the budgetary process in the United States[12] and his conjecture that one could rationalize that process as an incrementalist one, Davis, Dempster, and Wildavsky (henceforth DDW) have formulated an econometric model which reduces the multilevel and complex structure of the budgetary process in the American federal government to two basic relationships.[13] The first states that the appropriations requested by any agency through the Bureau of the Budget is a fixed proportion of the appropriations accepted by Congress for that agency in the previous year plus a random component. This relationship can be summarized as

$$A_{bt} = \beta_b E_{bt-1} + v_{bt} \tag{9.3}$$

where A_{bt} are the requested appropriations of agency of bureau b in period t, E_{bt-1}, the appropriations passed the year before,

11.   In Appendix 2, I examine some empirical regularities discovered by other students of the public sector, regularities that are not dissimilar to the ones studied in this section.

12.   A. Wildavsky, *The Politics of the Budgetary Process* (Little, Brown & Co., 1964).

13.   O. A. Davis, M. A. H. Dempster, and A. Wildavsky, "A Theory of the Budgetary Process," *American Political Science Review* (September 1966), pp. 529–47, and "On the Process of Budgeting: An Empirical Study of Congressional Appropriations," *Papers on Non-Market Decision-Making*, I. ed. G. Tullock, (Charlottesville, Va: University of Virginia Press, 1966) pp. 63–132. DDW test a number of strategies for each of the two aggregate bodies. For expositional reasons I limit myself to the two relationships that have been found to be most fruitful.

and v_{bt} a random variable with an expected value of zero and an unknown finite variance. As it stands, equation (9.3) collapses the two agencies studied—the Bureau of the Budget and the entire executive branch of government—into one hypothetical or putative body.

The second relationship asserts that congressional requested appropriations in a given year are a fixed proportion of the requested appropriations of that year plus a random component, so that

$$E_{bt} = a_b A_{bt} + \eta_{bt} \qquad (9.4)$$

where E and A have the same meaning as above and η_{bt} is another random component with zero mean and unknown finite variance. Again, all congressional committees, both of the House of Representatives and of the Senate, are collapsed into one body. Both (9.3) and (9.4) are surrogate functions in that they do not pretend to describe in detail the behavior of the bodies involved, but limit themselves to asserting that they behave as if they were governed by these two equations.

By combining (9.3) and (9.4), one obtains

$$E_{bt} = k_b E_{bt-1} + \varepsilon_{bt} \qquad (9.5)$$

which describes the behavior of the system. It is not necessary to go into the estimating procedures used nor into the methods utilized by DDW to discover whether (9.3) and (9.4) are stable relationships since this is well done in their papers; it suffices to say that when applied to actual data, the equation produces very good results, though they are marked by what DDW call shift-points, that is by breaks or discontinuities in the basic relationships. These shift-points are illustrated in figure 9.1. Located at t_1, t_2, and t_3 where breaks appear in the curve, they are in effect new curves whose origin is at zero, but for some purposes they can be thought of as describing a constant underlying process.

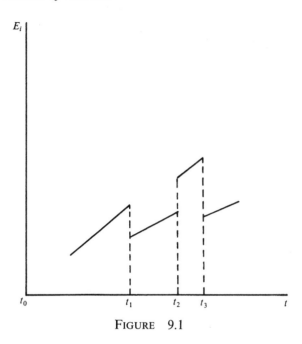

FIGURE 9.1

DDW have not provided a rigorous explanation for these shift-points, nor by inference have they provided a very rigorous explanation for the constancy of a, β, and k for the periods over which they are constant, unless the incrementalist hypothesis is taken to be a rigorous explanation.

Before discussing these issues, we must ask whether (9.3)–(9.5) which were developed for the American congressional systems can be used in parliamentary systems of the British or Canadian varieties. Beyond the problem of the availability of data, which is more serious in the latter systems, there is the question of the extent to which DDW-type models correctly represent the type of strategy game that goes on in parliamentary systems. I wish to suggest that as surrogate models they would probably perform fairly well, though they would have to be seen as surrogate of different real models. The differences in the surrogate models between the two types of political systems would appear as differences in the size of the a's and of the β's and as differences in the frequency and location of the shift-points. One problem with this view is that it is not easy to verify since data to estimate (9.3) is not directly available in parliamentary systems. However, given that (9.5) can be estimated and given that a in (9.4) is likely to be in the neighborhood of 1 in parliamentary systems—an assumption that can be verified—one could still obtain a measure of β, since if $a = 1$, β will be equal to k (except for random components) and hence the model could still be applicable. The crux of the matter for this applicability in parliamentary systems is an independent estimation of the value of a. In the remainder of this study, I assume that the model developed by DDW can be extended to parliamentary and to other types of systems.

4.   The Theory and the Evidence

We must now ask ourselves whether the hypothesis suggested in the two first sections of this chapter can be reconciled with the evidence of the third section. There are two different problems: first, that of explaining the constancy of k over fairly long stretches of time and second, that of providing an explanation for the frequency, size, and location of shift-points. If we restrict ourselves to the theory of bureaucracy advanced above, there is not very much that can be said about the second problem, but the behavior of a, β, and k in the range over which they are constant implies something about the cost of anti-distortion devices and behavior of bargaining. Indeed, it tells us that over these ranges these variables are constant or that they move in opposite directions in such a way as to cancel each other out.

If we neglect the cost of anti-distortion devices, the unchanging bargaining pattern between politicians and bureaucrats and between bureaucrats and bureaucrats can be understood in one of two complementary ways. It may simply be that bargaining strength or bargaining power does not change so that in the final outcome the relative position of each bureau in the structure of bureaus is unaltered vis-à-vis politicians and vis-à-vis other bureaus. A situation of this kind would imply that a, β, and k were constant. It would not tell us whether k was equal to, larger, or smaller than one, only that it did not change.

The second way of looking at the constancy of a, β, and k is consistent with some ex ante potential variations in bargaining strength, but assumes that the costs of moving from one state of the world to another is so high that the process of bargaining is reduced to simple rules of thumb whereby the appropriations of this year are increased (or reduced or maintained) over those of last year by the same proportion as those of last year had been increased (or reduced or maintained) over those of the year before.[14] In other words, alterations in any rule of conduct or in any important variable are costly; consequently, changes that lead to variations in the position of bureaus are conducive to strife and to the disruption of the internal organizational rules of the institution and as a result will be engaged in as seldom as possible.

It is well to keep in mind, however, that k varies over agencies and departments, indicating that some bureaus are growing and some decaying at faster rates than others. If the bargaining strength of politicians is called σ_p and that of bureaucrats σ_b, the differences in the rate of growth of bureaus indicate

14. O. E. Williamson, "A Rational Theory of the Federal Budgetary Process," *in Papers on Non-Market Decision-Making*, II. ed. G. Tullock, (Charlottesville, Va: University of Virginia Press, 1966) pp. 71–90.

that σ_b/σ_p varies over government agencies and departments. We have seen that variations in k produce shift-points in the linear decision-rules of DDW. Some proportion of these variations can be accounted for by changes in σ_b/σ_p. As a consequence, equation (9.5) could be rewritten as

$$E_{bt} = k_b(\sigma_{bt}/\sigma_{pt})E_{bt-1} + \varepsilon_{bt} \qquad (9.6)$$

which provides us with part—but only part—of an explanation for the shift-points portrayed in figure 13.

If we aggregate over bureaus (agencies and departments), we let

$$E_t = \sum_b E_{bt} \qquad (9.7)$$

and

$$k = \sum w_b k_b \qquad (9.8)$$

(where w_b is the weight or relative importance of each bureau in the structure), and if in addition we write B_t as the vector or relative bargaining strengths $(\sigma_{bt}/\sigma_{bt})$, we can write an aggregate version of (9.6) as

$$E_t = k(B_t)\,E_{t-1} + \varepsilon_t{}^1 \qquad (9.9)$$

Now if we observe that $k > 1$, this must imply that the budget of the government is growing in the aggregate either because tax rates are higher or, with given tax rates, because tax bases are being broadened or, with given tax rates and tax bases, because of a positive rate of economic growth or, with a zero rate of growth and progressive tax rates, because of inflation.

In this and the last section, I have been running slightly ahead of my story in that I have been discussing applications of an incompletely formulated model, but given the way the DDW hypothesis is presented this was an appropriate digression. In concluding this chapter, I should, however, repeat a point that

I will emphasize again in the next chapter: on the supply side of the public sector, the dominant force in shaping the pattern of expenditure policies and tax-prices is the relative power of politicians and bureaucrats. If one had to write a supply function for the public sector, one should then write

$$S^g = f(Q, B) \tag{9.10}$$

where, it will be recalled, Q stands for the vector of tax-prices and B is equal to σ_b/σ_p, the ratio of the power of bureaucrats to that of politicians; and where the superscript g indicates that (9.10) is a supply function.

Some readers may wonder why Q has been introduced in the supply function since clearly the government cannot be assumed to be a competitive supplier. My excuse for placing that vector in the equation is to remind us that all the adjustments needed on the supply side are determined by the coercion felt by citizens and hence by the interaction between S and Q, that is by the interactions between the quantity of public policies supplied and their tax-prices. I return to this question in the next two chapters.

IV

Resource Allocation in the Public Sector

Our People's Government is one that genuinely represents the people's
interests, it is a government that serves the people. Nevertheless,
there are still certain contradictions between the government and the
people. These include contradictions among the interests of the
state, the interests of the collective and the interests of the individual;
between democracy and centralism; between the leadership and the led;
and the contradiction arising from the bureaucratic style of work
of certain government workers in their relations with the masses.

MAO TSE-TUNG

10

The Equilibrium Quantity of Government Policies

1.   Introduction

We are now in a position to bring together the building blocks developed in the previous chapters. On the demand side, these include the preferences of citizens for public policies as these are related to the incomes of citizens and to the tax-prices that have to be paid for these policies as well as to the costs of using the various instruments of political participation that can lead to the desired supply of public expenditure and taxation policies. On the supply side, there is the degree of competition to which the opposition submits the governing party and the degree of interest which this competition stimulates in citizens as reflected in what they remember of the disparities between the weights attached to their tastes by politicians and the weights they themselves use; there is also the bargaining strengths of politicians and bureaucrats which determine the instruments used by politicians in their efforts to reduce the degree of coercion placed on some citizens and the policies that will be implemented.

To analyze how these various factors interact to determine the equilibrium supply of public output, I will examine three cases which together comprise most possible situations.[1] The first arises when the level of political participation costs (p^*) is such that the number (or proportion) (N_p) of citizens who make their preferences known to the governing party is larger than the number (or proportion) (N_r) which the decision-rule in force dictates should support the governing party if this latter is to be reelected. This is a situation that will arise when p^* is low. The second situation that I will examine is when p^* is high and consequently when $N_p < N_r$, and finally I will discuss a particular situation that arises when p^* is such that $N_p = N_r$.

To put it differently, I assume, following the discussion of chapter 6, that ceteris paribus the extent of political participation increases as the cost of political participation falls, a phenomenon that can be portrayed by the negatively sloped curve in figure 10.1. In that figure the abscissa measures not the absolute number of citizens who use the instruments of political action and thus make their preferences known to the governing party and seek to influence it as in figure 6.3 of chapter 6 (N_p), but that number as a ratio of the number that the decision-rule requires should support the governing party if it is to be reelected.

The decision to proceed with the analysis as if political participation costs could be aggregated in one variable simplifies the analysis, but, as the discussion of chapter 6 should have made clear, does not subtract anything essential from it. Furthermore, many of those who use the instruments of political action are not themselves individual citizens, but may be corporate bodies. In this case, as always when dealing with corporations, an assumption must be made about the relationship that is supposed to exist between the corporate body or

1.   In the next chapter I examine how the system adjusts when external disturbances alter the basic data of the problem.

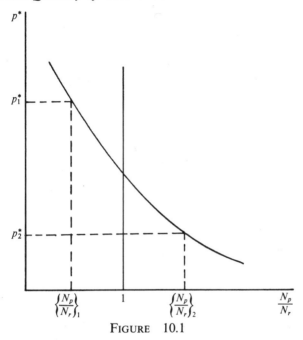

FIGURE   10.1

its managers and the members of the institution. The simplest assumption to make, and the one made here, is that managers will not seek to influence politicians in a way that is detrimental to the interest of their shareholders or members.

Returning to figure 10.1, note that at $N_p/N_r = 1$, the vertical line divides the plane in two (not usually equal) areas: one where $N_p/N_r < 1$, that is, where $N_r > N_p$ and p^* is high (i.e., p_1^*), and one where $N_p/N_r > 1$ and p^* is low (i.e., p_2^*). The position of the solid vertical line (where $N_p/N_r = 1$) will change if there are changes in the decision-rules used in a given society.[2] Given these definitions, we can now analyze each case separately.

2.   I examine the effect of such a change in the next chapter.

2. Low Political Participation Costs

To proceed with the analysis of the case when $N_p/N_r > 1$ (that is when $N_p > N_r$), I assume first that the level of competition provided by the opposition party (or parties) and by other opposing forces in society is constant; and second, that even if the governing party can adopt new policy instruments and discard some that are already in use, it will not use any instrument that does not have an accounting counterpart. As a consequence, changes in the accounting budget will always be changes in the economic one. Furthermore, I assume that tax-prices and incomes do not change. The justification for this assumption is that given the level of p^*, changes in tax-prices and incomes will have the effect of changing the demand for public output exactly as described in chapter 6. Nothing new would be added by assuming that they change.

When $N_p > N_r$, the number of citizens who try to influence politicians by using some or all of the political instruments examined in chapter 5 is larger than the number whose preferences must be satisfied if the governing party is to be reelected. This implies that the governing party has the freedom to select from the set of all citizens whose preferences are signaled, one subset and neglect the others. This, in turn, implies that the governing party has the freedom to implement a bundle of policies that satisfy the preferences of a number of citizens no smaller than N_r and disregard other policies and still be reelected.

To see this more clearly, consider the following array of v policy bundles, each one of which is made up of n policies. One can imagine S_{11} (policy 1 in bundle 1) to be a clean-air policy, S_{21} to be police protection, S_{31}, national defense, and so on for all possible policies. Not all policies making up bundle 1 need be implemented at a point in time, so that S_{11} or S_{51}

could be zero. The policies that make up bundle 1 should therefore be thought of as being a given level or scale of policies 1, 2, . . . *n*. The policies in bundle 2, therefore, differ from the policies in bundle 1 only in the level of implementation. If, for example, S_{41} is the amount of public transportation that one supplies with $1.00 of expenditures, S_{42} is the amount attainable when expenditures are increased to $1.10 or reduced to 90¢ (assuming constant average cost).

$$
\begin{array}{cccc|ccc}
S_{11} & S_{12} & \ldots & S_{1k} & S_{1k+1} & \ldots & S_{1v} \\
S_{21} & S_{22} & \ldots & S_{2k} & S_{2k+1} & & S_{2v} \\
\cdot & \cdot & \cdot & \cdot & & \cdot \\
\cdot & \cdot & \cdot & \cdot & & \cdot \\
\cdot & \cdot & \cdot & \cdot & & \cdot \\
S_{n1} & S_{n2} & \ldots & S_{nk} & S_{nk+1} & & S_{nv}
\end{array}
$$

The policy bundles in the table are divided in two classes: the first class comprises all the bundles labeled from 1 to k, while the second is made up of bundles $k + 1$ to v. Let us call the first subset K and the second one V. The bundles that make up K have in common that the implementation of any one of them would insure the governing party's reelection. In other words, bundle 1 is such that at the existing level and structure of tax rates, at least N_r citizens would support the governing party, and since N_r is the number required for reelection, the governing party would be reelected. The difference between bundle 1 and bundle 2 is that if 2 is implemented there will still be N_r citizens who will support the governing party, but they will not be the same citizens as when bundle 1 is implemented.

Let me reemphasize the point with a numerical example. Imagine a society made up of 7 citizens called 1, 2, 3, . . . , and suppose that the support of any 4 will insure reelection.

If p^*—the level of political participation cost—is such that 5 (numbers 1, 2, 3, 4, and 5) citizens signal their preferences to the governing party, this latter can select any 4 out of these 5, satisfy their preferences, and be reelected. Now suppose that citizens 1, 2, 3, and 4 would support the government if bundle 1 is implemented; that 1, 2, 3, and 5 would support it if bundle 2 is implemented; that 2, 3, 4, and 5 favor bundle 3; that 1, 2, 4, 5 desire bundle 4; and that 1, 3, 4 and 5 want bundle k. The question facing us therefore is: which of these bundles will be implemented?

This numerical example also makes clear that the size of class K is determined by the number of degrees of freedom that the excess of N_p over N_r allows, that is, by the extent to which the height of p^* permits the number of citizens who reveal their preferences to the governing party to exceed the number which the decision-rules dictate is required for the reelection of the governing party.

On the other hand, the bundles of policies which make up class V are such that the implementation of any one of them would insure defeat of the governing party at the next election. To answer the question asked above, we must in effect answer two interrelated questions: why would a party ever choose a bundle in V? and if it chooses one in K, which one will it be? To put it differently, can one specify the forces and their interplay that will lead to the selection of one particular bundle in K out of the full set of policy bundles? The answer I wish to suggest is that the bundle that will be chosen will be largely determined by bargaining between politicians and bureaucrats and hence will be largely dependent on bargaining power. We can usefully distinguish two cases: one that obtains when the preferences of bureaucrats for policies can be satisfied by one of the policy bundles in K, and the other when these preferences dictate a bundle belonging to the subset V.

If the preferences of bureaucrats can be met by a policy bundle in K, then the supply of public policies at any point of time is immediately given at least as long as only one bundle in K can satisfy the preferences of bureaucrats. If there is more than one such bundle—that is, if there are a number of bundles in K between which bureaucrats are indifferent because all imply the same relative size of bureaus—politicians will have unused degrees of freedom at their disposal and they will be able to use them to pursue any goal they choose as long as these goals are not detrimental or in conflict with their reelection. Returning to equation (7.1)—namely $U_p = U_p(\pi, a_m)$—the foregoing argument says that, given $\pi \geq \pi^*$ (a value of π that is deemed to insure reelection), politicians will set some a_m's at positive level to use up the degrees of freedom at their disposal.

To repeat: when $N_p > N_r$ and when bureacrats are satisfied, politicians, having insured a level of π which they think is safe, will proceed to implement some policies that will produce some $a_m > 0$ and therefore will implement some policies that will in general be at variance with the preferences of citizens.[3] From this we see that given non-unanimity decision rules, non-zero election period, and/or some full-line supply, reductions in p^*—the cost of political participation—will increase N_p relative to N_r and thus make it easier for politicians to implement policies at variance with the preferences of citizens. Though reform-minded citizens may wish to achieve lower p^*, it must be emphasized that this will reduce the power of politicians only to the extent that N_r can also be increased either by changing the decision-rules so that they will approach

3.   I neglect the trivial case that obtains when increasing a given a also increases π. This case is trivial in view of the definition of the a's. Recall that these refer to variables that lead to improvements in the private wealth and prestige of politicians.

unanimity or by changing the length of the election period by making it approach zero and/or by reducing the extent of full-line supply.

At the same time, if the number of policy bundles in K that satisfy the preferences of bureaucrats is larger than one, and if these policy bundles do not satisfy these preferences equally well, the chosen bundle will be determined through (implicit or explicit) bargaining between bureaucrats and politicians. The latter will want a bundle such that $U_p(\pi, a_m)$ is made as large as possible, while the former will want the bundle that will maximize the relative size of their bureaus. The outcome will be the product of the relative bargaining power of the two parties.

On the other hand, if the objective of bureaucrats—the maximization of the relative size of their bureaus—can only be achieved by the selection of a policy bundle in V, as may sometimes be the case, a conflict will arise. Whether a bundle in V or one in K will be chosen will depend on relative bargaining power.

Since bargaining power plays such an important role in the public sector, it is important that a few more words be added to the concept even if a full theory cannot be adumbrated at this stage of our knowledge. Bargaining strength or power is a form of capital: one can accumulate power or disinvest some of it. Like capital, therefore, it is a scarce resource. It is capital also in the sense that investment in it represents a subtraction from current consumption broadly defined. I once heard someone say of a third person: "he is too selfish to wish to be powerful." That proposition well summarizes the idea that there is an alternative cost to accumulating power and hence bargaining strength.

To invest in power is costly of material resources but also

of time and energy since some of these must be used to create dependence in others. It is also costly since power can principally be augmented by acquiring information, by insuring that the same (or substitute) information will not be acquired by others, and by releasing the smallest amount of information possible whenever some has to be given up. As the preceding discussion emphasized, the power of politicians (relative to that of bureaucrats) can also be increased by reductions in the level of p^* and thus by altering the relative sizes of the K and V policy bundles.

It should be clear by now that the discussion of the last chapter relating to control-loss and to the behavior of bureaus was in effect a discussion of the technology and of the process of the accumulation of power for the purpose—as we see in this chapter—of achieving the implementation of the policy bundle most congruent with the objective function of bureaucrats.[4]

To summarize the main points of this section, one can recall that when $N_p > N_r$, the policy bundle that will be selected for implementation will depend on the relative bargaining strength of bureaucrats and politicians. If the politicians are more powerful, they will select a bundle in subset K that will insure their reelection and meet the preferences of bureaucrats to the extent feasible. If, on the other hand, bureaucrats are more powerful, they will allow a bundle in K to be selected if this is consistent with achieving the largest possible relative size for their bureau, otherwise they will select a bundle in subset V and force the governing party to be defeated at the polls.

---

4.   It is sometimes possible for bureaus to act as lobbies or to obtain the support of lobbies and hence to acquire more power. This usually happens when former bureaucrats become the representative of lobbies or when lobby personnel become bureaucrats—both observable phenomena.

3. High Political Participation Costs

When $N_p < N_r$, the number of citizens using the instruments of political action falls short of the number whose preferences must be satisfied if the governing party is going to be reelected, and, as a consequence, the governing party does not, initially at least, know what policy bundle to implement. Such a situation means that the governing party must decide on the provision of policies knowing that these will not meet the preferences of a sufficiently large fraction of the electorate to enable it to regain office at the end of the election period. It is well to reflect on the meaning of this situation: some citizens will surely use the instruments of political action and signal their preferences. But by construction the number that can so reveal their preferences is too small for the governing party to be returned to office with their support only. As a consequence, a large number of citizens will in general be coerced so that when the election period runs to its end they will, if one of the opposition parties proposes an acceptable platform—that is, a platform that would reduce the extent of coercion—vote for that party.

Note, however, that since p^* is such that $N_r > N_p$ the nongoverning party (or parties) will probably have less knowledge of the preferences of citizens, and certainly not more, than the governing one has. All parties and politicians will in these circumstances engage extensively in search activities in the hope that such activities will improve their knowledge of the preferences of citizens and make their reelection or election easier. Competition between parties, though it will partly consist of marginal adjustments in platforms, will to a very large extent be concentrated on the business of eking out knowledge of the preferences of citizens. This task will be easier if the electoral system is such that the support of only a few citizens is required for reelection as was the case in the United Kingdom before the extension of the franchise in 1867 (and again in 1884 and to women in 1918 and 1928).

Indeed, if the number of citizens required for reelection is absolutely small, it may be possible through search to discover fairly well what the preferences of these citizens are. As the franchise is extended—itself a phenomenon that may come about because the governing party knows or thinks it knows the preferences of persons which are not yet members of the electorate—the techniques of search will become more elaborate and more extensive, in particular if the costs of using these techniques are also falling.[5] In fact, a cursory perusal of the literature yields the impression that the franchise was extended in response to a reduction in the cost of search and hence in the cost of ascertaining the preferences of citizens made possible by the introduction and refinement of the various techniques and methods of measuring preferences and public opinion.

Furthermore, when $N_p < N_r$, governing and non-governing parties will engage in a large amount of advertising in an effort to homogenize the preferences of the electorate and thus make it easier to ascertain what they are. With the diffusion of the press and of the other mass media, the costs of political advertising have greatly been reduced and the task of the political parties partly simplified.

The effect of search and advertising is to convert an unfavorable situation—where $N_p < N_r$—to one resembling a favorable one, where $N_p > N_r$. Once this point has been recognized, it becomes clear that a governing party can also engage in search and advertising even when $N_p > N_r$ if by so

5. For a discussion of this process of competition in the British context, see T. W. Hutchison's excellent and fascinating "Markets and the Franchise," London: *Institute of Economic Affairs* (Occasional Paper no. 10, 1966).

doing it can increase the number of degrees of freedom at its disposal and in this way make it easier for itself to pursue goals unrelated to that of its reelection and hence to the preferences of some citizens.

Besides engaging in search and advertising when $N_p < N_r$ (or for that matter $N_p > N_r$), governing parties can implement legislation aimed at directly reducing p^*, the cost of political participation, and thus transforming a N_p that is smaller than N_r into one that is larger (or into one that is much larger). In seeking to achieve this goal, they can, for example, legalize the existence of lobbies and of many activities or pressure groups; they can allow the expenses of running lobbies, of political mobility, of engaging in political pressures, of seeking redress in the courts, or even of political bribes to be deducted from income (or from some other magnitudes) in computing tax liabilities; they can also reduce police and other law enforcement activities where political behaviors such as social movements, illegal self-provision of public policies, and the actions of small pressure groups are involved All of these actions have the effect of lowering p^* and of increasing the value of N_p relative to N_r.

4.   A Limiting Case

When $N_p = N_r$, the number of citizens whose preferences are signaled to the governing party is exactly equal to the number whose preferences must be satisfied if the governing party is going to be reelected. Given this state of affairs—and assuming as always that the distribution of citizens over electoral constituencies is the one that will insure reelection of the governing party—that party has no freedom in choosing policies save that of selecting the bundle that will reduce to zero the degree of coercion imposed on these N_r citizens. It will achieve this end by optimally adjusting the tax bases, the tax rates, the tax exemptions, the deductions, the loopholes, the subsidies— those paid in money and those paid in kind—the probability of apprehending these citizens if they break the law, and if they are apprehended the level of fines and other punishments, and finally by optimally adjusting the level of policies themselves, of their substitutes and complements, to the preferences of these citizens.

Given a level of p^* such that $N_p = N_r$, it is not the politicians nor the bureaucrats that select the citizens—and hence the set of preferences—that will be satisfied. In a manner of speaking, it is the citizens themselves who do the selection. In this case, therefore, if political participation costs are principally money costs, the group of citizens whose preferences will be revealed to the governing party will depend directly on the distribution of money income, and the policies implemented by the governing party will therefore tend to reflect the distribution of money income. Chances are that in such a society the political system will mostly reflect the preferences of the higher income group in the population. To the superficial observer, such a system will appear to be corrupt, while in fact the system is one that operates with no degree of freedom and therefore one that must constantly adjust to the preferences of the relevant citizens.

On the other hand if political participation costs are mostly time and energy costs, the groups whose preferences are represented will also depend on the distribution of money income though only indirectly; but in such a system it is probably the preferences of lower income groups that will be revealed.

In a political system in which $N_r = N_p$, the number of policy bundles in the subset K of bundles that insure the reelection of the governing party is equal to one. Though bureaucrats may not want that bundle and hence force the governing party to an electoral defeat, the party itself will, in maximizing Up (π, a_m), set all the a's equal to zero and single-mindedly pursue the objective of its reelection. Whether the party is defeated or reelected will depend on relative bargaining strengths, unless bureaucrats are satisfied with the policy bundle in subset K.

If we drop some of the assumptions made earlier and instead assume unanimity to be the prevailing decision-rule, the election period to be zero, and no full-line supply, but still have $N_r = N_p$, then the traditional welfare economist's conclusions about Pareto optimality still hold, but loopholes, exemptions, credits, discriminatory subsidies, etc., have to be interpreted as additions to or subtractions from the tax-price which would be, once modified, exactly equal to benefit tax rates for public output.[6]

5.　A Short Normative Digression

One of the most basic problems of welfare economics and one that has plagued that field of inquiry since its very beginning is that of finding out whether non-market organization leads to over- or to underinvestment in some activities. If the analysis presented in this chapter is correct, the extent of over- or under-investment will depend principally on the level of political participation costs and on the relative bargaining power of bureaucrats and politicians. Since these magnitudes vary over government departments, one should not be surprised, once the

6.　It should be clear to the reader at this point in the argument that to assume unanimity, zero length election periods and no full-line supply is tantamount to assuming the elimination of representative government. References to the "traditional welfare economist's conclusions about Pareto-optimality" in the text above cannot therefore be interpreted to say that a Pareto solution of the traditional kind is the desired solution.

politically desirable level of these variables had been found, to discover that in practice there is overinvestment in some activities and underinvestment in others. Only a view of the world that has no institutional counterpart can arrive at a simple un-ambiguous conclusion applicable to all activities.

11

Comparative Statical
Displacements of Equilibrium

1. Introduction

Having analyzed the forces that operate to determine the equilibrium supply of and demand for public policies in the last chapter, I will now examine how the public sector adjusts to external disturbances. It will be recalled that in previous discussions and especially in chapter 2 a large number of public policies were examined and were shown to be analyzable within one broad frame of reference. As a consequence, it will be sufficient if, in this chapter, I arbitrarily select two cases to examine the various possible disturbances to which the system may be subjected and to illustrate how the model works.

The first disturbance is a change in the level of unemployment in the economy. The problem will be discussed on the assumption that citizens—or at least a significant fraction of them—include the level of unemployment in their utility function. The second external disturbance is that of an exogenous change in the institutional framework that defines the rules of the game in the public sector. I will examine the effect of extending the franchise to a larger portion of the population. The analysis of this section—section 3 below—which examines a specific change in the decision-rules governing collective choices, is representative of the kind of analysis that would be conducted to examine changes in the length of the election period, in the degree of full-line supply, and in the costs of using the constitution.

The last section of the chapter presents a formal summary of the model in a way that makes it relatively easy to use the theory developed in this study to analyze statistical phenomena.

2. The Level of Unemployment

No society is permanently characterized by high or by low political participation costs, except relative to a given configuration of coercion. To put it differently, the level of political participation costs uniquely determines the extent of political participation only for a given distribution of the electorate's preferences for public policies, for a given institutional framework, for a given bundle of tax and expenditure policies, and hence for a given distribution of coercion over the electorate. When that distribution changes as a result of changes in the above mentioned data, the behavior of citizens and that of politicians, political parties, and bureaucrats will also change and thus lead to changes in the flow of public output, even though the costs of political participation (p_i^*) do not themselves change.

Assuming that all other policies are supplied in optimal quantities, we can examine the above problem by considering what would happen in a society if the level of unemployment increased as a result of an external disturbance. Suppose that initially the vector of p_i^*'s was prohibitively high, i.e., was so high that the number of citizens signaling their preferences to the governing party (N_p) was substantially below the number required by the decision-rules if that party is to be reelected

(N_r), and suppose also that after the increase in unemployment and hence after the increase in coercion, the vector of p_i*'s is still prohibitively high. In these circumstances the level of unemployment would not immediately be reduced, though if the cost of voting is low, the governing party would be defeated on election day and replaced by the opposition.

To proceed with this analysis, we must really distinguish between the cost of voting $(p_v{}^*)$ and the cost of the other political instruments $(p_{i_*v}{}^*)$. If we hold to the assumption that the $p_{i_*v}{}^*$ are prohibitively high—as this term is defined above—both before and after the increase in unemployment, but that $p_v{}^*$ is sufficiently low that on election day $N_p > N_r$, then citizens will vote *against* the governing party.[1] Because the supply of all other policies is assumed to be optimal, the opposition would learn as a result of its election to office that the level of unemployment is too high and that it should reduce it. There is no reason, given the nature of the problem, to suppose, however, that it would reduce it to the desired level and hence it would probably itself be defeated at the subsequent election. The return of the former governing party would again bring the system closer to the desired level. Only when that level was achieved would this pendulum process stop.

We can clarify and extend the above argument with the help of figure 11.1, which is a slight modification of figure 6.3. As a result of the increase in the level of unemployment from U_0 to U_1—the cost of the policy instruments used to generate an employment level equal to $(1 - U_0)$ remaining unchanged at q_0—the extent of coercion increases by an amount that is represented by the triangle labeled a in panel A. As a consequence, the political participation curve shifts from $n_{i_*v}{}^1$ to $n_{i_*v}{}^2$ but

1. They cannot vote *for* an opposition party since, given the assumed level of $p_{j_*v}{}^*$ the opposition cannot be imagined to know that citizens are coerced any more than the governing party can.

Panel A

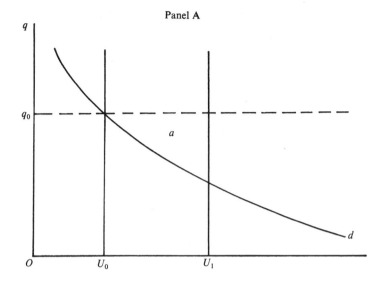

Panel B

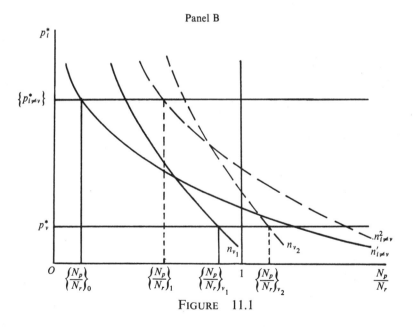

FIGURE 11.1

given the height of $p_{i+v}*$ at $(p_{i+v}*)^1$, the number of citizens who reveal their preference relative to those required for reelection remains such that $(N_p/N_r) < 1$. In a situation such as this one, U_1 becomes the politically acceptable level of unemployment, at least until the next election. Then, however, if the level of p_v* is such that on the participation curve n_{v-2} in panel B$(N_p/N_r) > 1$, the governing party will be defeated and the opposition—now the new government—will seek to reduce the level of unemployment. The pendulum process described above is not represented in figure 11.1, but we have already seen that it will only stop when U_0 has been achieved.

In the preceding analysis, I assumed throughout that all policies, except the level of employment, were optimally supplied so that the only policy to generate coercion was the level of unemployment. If the number of policies that are non-optimally adjusted as a result of external disturbances is greater than one, this will simply imply that the pendulum problem described above will last longer. Indeed, in a system in which $(N_p/N_r) < 1$ and where p_v* is low, equilibrium will be approached only very slowly; the lags will depend on the length of the election period, on the size of the adjustment toward equilibrium in each period, and on the number of policies that are not optimally supplied.

If the increase in unemployment and hence in coercion is such that the participation curve shifts to a level so that $(N_p/N_r) > 1$, the governing party will wish to engage in policies to reduce the level of unemployment to U_0. It will engage in these policies if it has the cooperation of the bureaucrats or, in the absence of that support, if its bargaining strength relative to that of the bureaucrats is sufficient to insure that the desired policy be implemented.

The bureaucracy could, of course, be indifferent about the level of employment, but have very definite preferences about the policy instruments that should be used and those that should not to combat unemployment. It is easy to imagine and simple to document that bureaucrats may have preferences for instruments that are technically non-apposite. If the bureaucrats have enough power (relative to that of politicians) to force the governing party to use its preferred policy instruments, unemployment will not be reduced and the party will be defeated at the election and replaced by an opposition party. Should the new governing party not have the power to force its bureaucrats to use the instruments that will reduce unemployment, it will itself be defeated at the next election. Again we would have a pendulum movement, but one which, given the terms of the discussion, does not tend to an equilibrium.

There is no reason to believe that the pendulum movement would persist at least if there are policies which are substitutes for employment, such as labor retraining programs, welfare schemes, etc. Instead of facing a defeat imposed by the bureaucrats, a governing party would seek to implement some of these substitute policies. It would choose those substitute policies which would meet the preferences of the bureaucrats and hence which would be very labor intensive. In addition, the governing party would try to select those substitute policies which make discriminatory differential adjustments, as described in chapter 8, possible.

3.   The Extension of the Franchise

The mechanics of adjustment described in the last chapter and in the foregoing section should now be clear, and, as a consequence, I will in this section only briefly indicate how the system adjusts to yet another external disturbance. Principally, I will describe the changes in the configuration of coercion that is likely if the franchise is extended. Such an exercise is useful in itself, but it will also serve to illustrate one of the more profound changes that have historically influenced the pattern of government expenditure and taxation in democratic countries.

We can begin the analysis by considering a society made up of three groups: a first group of younger individuals aged 18 to 21 who are largely unproductive in that they do not earn any taxable income, a second group that is productive, and a third group of also unproductive (in the sense, in this case, that they do not earn non-property income), retired individuals. Let us label these groups I, II and III. If we begin by assuming that only group II has been enfranchised, we will observe, given the other features of the institutional framework, the structures of tax-prices, the level of income, the level of political participation costs, and the relative power of politicians and bureaucrats, a given pattern of taxation and expenditure policies, and we will also observe, because group II citizens are the only ones paying taxes on labor incomes, that a relevant number of them (a number defined by the decision-rules in force) will require, if they are to continue to extend their support to the governing party, that this latter supplies a particular bundle of policies.

Imagine that the franchise is now extended to group III. This will have the effect of changing the pattern of coercion in the electorate. First, these new citizens will not be paying taxes on labor income since they are not earning that kind of income and they will not earn any in the future; they will, however, be paying taxes on their purchases and on their wealth and property since all of them will be buying goods and services and some of them will own wealth and property. As a consequence, they will have a preference for income over sales, property, and wealth taxes; if the total of their income from property and other taxable assets is lower than the income from similar sources for group II citizens, they will favor progressive taxation of these incomes, otherwise they will prefer proportional or even regressive taxation, as now exists for land and real estate; finally, if they are less wealthy than group II citizens, they will favor expenditure policies which transfer real income to them, such as old age pensions, retirement plans, free medical care for the aged, and similar schemes.

Whether their preferences will lead to changes in the supply of policies will depend, among other things, on the relative importance of group III in the electorate and on the extent to which the welfare of group III enters the utility functions of citizens in group II; in most circumstances the first of these factors is likely to dominate. As a result, unless all citizens in group II have the same utility functions as those in group III, catering to the preferences of citizens in II will generate coercion in group III, and vice versa. A completely new bundle of policies will be required if the governing party is to remain in office. Note that if group III citizens are poorer than those of group II, one is likely to observe, with the extension of the franchise, an increase in the size of the public sector; while if group III citizens are wealthier, the opposite is likely to occur.

The extension of the franchise to group I will not have the same effect since the individuals making up that group will soon be members of group II and, though they are currently unproductive and also can be expected to discount the effects of currently implemented policies on them, they cannot be assumed not to expect that these policies will not affect them. Consequently, the extension of the franchise to group I will be very different than its extension to group III. Indeed, one would expect the changes resulting from an extension to group I to have only marginal effect on government policies. That effect will not be zero, however, and in addition will represent a diffusion of, and hence a reduction in the power of, the already enfranchised groups. This may be the reason why extension to group I people is often opposed by group II and III citizens. In fact, group III should really oppose such extensions to the extent that the tastes of group I citizens resemble those of group II.

There is, however, another more subtle effect of the extension of the franchise. We can examine it by considering the difference between the situation that arises when, let us say 10 percent of the population is enfranchised, as was approximately the case in the United Kingdom during the nineteenth century, and another where 65 or 70 percent of the population is. When the enfranchised population is about 10 percent, the governing party can more easily implement discriminatory tax, subsidy, and other policies—and a smaller volume of them—than when the enfranchised population is 65 percent since the external effect—the fact that a subsidy (or other variables) to citizen A necessarily implies lower benefits or higher taxes for citizen B—of these policies is spread over a large fraction of the population that is not enfranchised (90 percent) and whose experienced coercion is of no direct and immediate import for the political process. To put the matter differently, with the extension of the franchise, the task of the government in designing discriminatory policies is made more difficult since the number of utility functions that have to be taken into account and not subjected to coercion through negative external effects is increased.[2]

2. There are other *complementary* forces at play. In a letter to me Gordon Tullock commented on the above proposition as follows: "It's apparently historically true that governments such as that of Venice or Berne where the franchised citizens, who are a very small and hereditary part of the entire population, functioned extremely well. An obvious advantage that these small groups of hereditary voters had was that they were deeply involved personally in the government and, hence, had motives to become rather well-informed. Further, they were, of course, trained from childhood in the 'politics' of the system. Thus you had a

4. The Empirical Analysis of Government Policies

It will be recalled that in the last section of chapter 6, I indicated that demand conditions could be summarized by an equation such as

$$S^d = g(Q, I, P_i{}^*) \tag{11.1}$$

where the superscript ^{d} to S insures that (11.1) be read as a demand function and where S is the flow of expenditure-type policies, Q is a vector of tax-prices, I is money income, and $P_i{}^*$ is a vector of political participation cost over citizens for the ith instrument.

Similarly, in chapter 9, I summarized supply conditions by

$$Sg = f(Q, B) \tag{11.2}$$

where, it will be recalled, B is equal to the ratio of the power of bureaucrats to that of politicians.

Now if we let E stand for the accounting or measured counterpart of the theoretically correct (S)-concept and if we interpret the Davis-Dempster-Wildavsky equation

$$E_t = k\, E_{t-1} + \varepsilon_t \tag{11.3}$$

---

relatively well-informed electorate which was broad enough so that the genetic factors which lead to morons occasionally becoming hereditary kings was not likely to be effective.

On the other hand, these groups were small enough so that they would be continuously in fear of non-democratic politics on the part of the rest of the citizenry. They could be overthrown at any time by those citizens who were not enfranchised, if those citizens organized themselves. The Venetian Senate and the Council of Berne of course, tried to raise the cost of organizing opposition, but they were never able to put it very high simply because they were such a very small minority. Under the circumstances, they were compelled to take into account the interests of the bulk of the population. No doubt, there was some exploitation of the non-enfranchised population, but of necessity, it would be small, Somewhat the same argument may apply to England before the **Reform Act** of 1830."

(where ε is a random variable with an expected value of zero and an unknown finite variance) to be a skelton or configuration of the reduced form of the structural model implicit in (11.1) and (11.2), together with the public sector clearance equation,

$$S^d = S^g \tag{11.4}$$

we can expand (11.3) to yield

$$E_t = k^* \{[B_t, Q_t], [h^*f(Q, I_t, P_{it}^*)], [\lambda_t]\} E_{t-1} + \varepsilon_t^* \tag{11.5}$$

where, from chapter 7, we recall that

$$h^* = \int_{t_1}^{t2} \rho_t(c_t)[r_c(t) - r_p(t)] \, dt \tag{11.6}$$

$(0 \leq \rho_t \leq 1)$, and where λ_t is a dummy variable taking the values of zero and one and indicating whether changes have taken place in the mix of accounting and economic policy instruments, and t is a time subscript; ρ_t is the memory factor; c_t, the degree of competition; and $r_c(t)$ and $r_p(t)$, the discount factors used by citizens and politicians respectively.

In applying (11.5) to government departments or to any subclass of expenditures, it may sometimes be desirable to drop I_t from (11.5) on the ground that its effect is already taken into account through E_{t-1}. But that is a practical question that would have to be resolved on practical grounds.

12

Conclusion

By now the reader of this book must be fully aware that I have simply applied conventional economic theory to representative government. Indeed, in the organization of the book itself I have carefully separated the forces that operate on the demand side of the public sector from those operating on the supply side and have taken special care to formulate the demand and supply problems in terms which depart as little as possible from conventional economic theory. I have then, as is traditional in that theory, examined the equilibrium of demand and supply as well as the nature of the process that yields comparative statical predictions.

The reader familiar with economic theory will have noted that at some crucial junctures I have had to introduce in the analysis some building blocks and some concepts that are alien to the standard theory of market behavior. The most important and most fundamental of these building blocks is the one that pertains to the characterization of the institutional framework. The reader will, indeed, have noticed that except for the peculiarities of public and non-private goods, the element that most strongly distinguishes the public from the competitive market sector is the institutional framework and, more specifically, what I have labeled the degrees of freedom that accrue to politicians because of the existence of election periods, non-unanimity decision-rules and full-line supply.

I have mentioned public and non-private goods. From the earliest years of my work on the problem of decision-making and resource allocation in the public sector, I have believed that it was very important to integrate, in an essential fashion, in the basic model of democracy formulated by Anthony Downs, those aspect of public goods which made it difficult to imagine that these goods would be supplied by anyone but governments. Consequently, both the demand and supply models have been formulated in such a way as to incorporate what I think are the dominant properties of public and non-private goods.

It should be mentioned that it is precisely in terms of these two features (impact of the degrees of freedom provided by the institutional framework and the characteristics of public goods) that this work departs most importantly from the classic work of Downs. To put it differently and more sharply, the institutional framework and the public aspect of many goods supplied by the government are able to account for many features of the real world that were accounted for by the cost of information in Downs' study.

The foregoing study has also tried to incorporate within the model of decision-making in the public sector one of the most prominent features of governmental structures, namely bureaucracy. As the reader will recall, the actions of bureaucrats had a real effect on the outcome of the model and as a consequence I incline to the view that models of the public sector which do not make a place for bureaus somehow miss something important. I wish to stress, however, that the exact role of the bureaucracy is still an open question. All classical political science is formulated without any mention of bureaus, and though this may reflect an oversight on the part of political scientists, it could also be that it is one of those very special assumptions, with which science is replete, which greatly simplify the task of understanding a phenomenon without neglecting anything important.

In short, the present study has been an effort to formulate a theory of representative government that would be capable of accounting for the data we possess on government expenditure and taxation patterns, while at the same time having a strong resemblance to economic theory, so that eventually it would be able to play the role that the theory of demand, the theory of supply, and the theory of markets play in helping us understand empirical phenomena.

Appendix 1

The Case of Non-private Goods

For any given quantity of a good X, let the following sum over j citizens

$$X = X_1 + X_2 + \cdots + X_J \qquad (A.1)$$

define a *private* good. Similarly, let

$$\bar{S} = S_1 + S_2 = \cdots = S_J \qquad (A.2)$$

define a pure *public* good.[1]

Now select a number a such that $0 < a \leq 1$) which describes the proportion of the benefits of a good that accrues to each of j citizens. We then have

$$
\begin{aligned}
E_1 &= a_1 \bar{S} \\
E_2 &= a_2 \bar{S} \\
&\quad \vdots \\
E_J &= a_J \bar{S}
\end{aligned}
\qquad (A.3)
$$

---

1. These are Samuelson's definitons; see "The Pure Theory of Public Expenditure," p. 387.

and if $a_1 = a_2 = \cdots = a_J$, we could write

$$E_1 = E_2 = \cdots = E_J = a \; \bar{S} \qquad (A.4)$$

both of which define a *non-private* good. Note that if $a = 1$ for all j's, (A.3) and (A.4) are identical to (A.2). It should be clear also that a need not be a scalar. Suppose that a function f can be found relating a to some variable such as distance or to any other variable, the definition of non-private goods given by (A.3) and (A.4) would be altered to

$$E_1 = f_1(a_1) \; \bar{S}$$
$$E_2 = f_2(a_2) \; \bar{S}$$
$$\cdot$$
$$\cdot \qquad\qquad\qquad (A.5)$$
$$\cdot$$
$$E_J = f_J(a_J) \; S$$

and to

$$E_1 = E_2 = \cdots = E_J = f(a) \; S \qquad (A.6)$$

Now assume the following utility functions:

$$U_1 = U_1(X_1, S) \qquad (A.7)$$

and $$\qquad U_2 = U_2(X_2, S) \qquad (A.8)$$

for two citizens only and in terms of one private and one public good only. Let the budget constraint facing the first citizen be

$$R_1 = X_1 + qS \qquad (A.9)$$

which q describes the ratio in which the tax burden is divided between the two citizens, that is the marginal tax-price of S. Let

$$R_2 = X_2 + (1 - q) \; S \qquad (A.10)$$

be the second citizens' budget constraint. Since $(0 < q < 1)$, the two constraints add up to

$$X_1 + X_2 + S = R \tag{A.11}$$

which is the society's national product.

By maximizing

$$G_1 = U_1(X_1, S) - \lambda(X_1 + qS - R_1) \tag{A.12}$$

formed with (A.7) and (A.9) and the undetermined lagrangean multiplier $\lambda(\neq 0)$, we get

$$q = \frac{U_1 S}{U_1 X_1} \tag{A.13}$$

where $\quad U_{1S} = \dfrac{\partial U_1}{\partial S}$ and $U_{1X_1} = \dfrac{\partial U_1}{\partial X_1}$.

Proceeding in a similar fashion for the second citizen, we calculate

$$1 - q = \frac{U_{2S}}{U_{2X_2}} \tag{A.14}$$

or $\quad q = 1 - \dfrac{U_{2S}}{U_{2X_2}}$

(A.13) and (A.14) define the equilibrium tax-prices for any quantity of S.

If (A.13) and (A.14) are summed, we obtain

$$\frac{U_{1s}}{U_{1X_1}} + \frac{U_{2S}}{U_{2X_2}} = 1 \tag{A.15}$$

which is the normative Pareto optimal solution, given the unitary marginal rate of transformation implicit in (A.11).[2]

Assume now that (A.7) and (A.8) are rewritten as

$$U_1 = U_1(X_1, aS) \tag{A.16}$$

and $\quad U_2 = U_2(X_2, aS) \tag{A.17}$

---

2. See note 1 above.

assuming for simplicity that $a_1 = a_2 = a$. If we maximize (A.16) subject to (A.9), we obtain

$$\frac{q}{a} = \frac{U_{1s}}{U_{1X_1}} \tag{A.18}$$

For the second citizen, maximizing (A.17) subject to (A.10) yields

$$(1 - q)\frac{1}{a} = \frac{U_{2s}}{U_{2X_2}} \tag{A.19}$$

(A.18) and (A.19) define the equilibrium tax-prices when non-private goods are supplied.

If we add (A.18) and (A.19), we get

$$\frac{U_{1S}}{U_{1X_1}} + \frac{U_{2S}}{U_{2X_2}} = \frac{1}{a} \tag{A.20}$$

and if the above simplification concerning a is dropped, we obtain

$$a_1\left(\frac{U_{1S}}{U_{1X_1}}\right) + a_2\left(\frac{U_{2S}}{U_{2X_2}}\right) = 1 \tag{A.21}$$

both of which describe the normative Pareto optimal solution when a non-private good is supplied.

If there are $i = 1, \ldots, N$ non-private goods, $k = 1, \ldots, K$ private goods and $j = 1, \ldots, J$ citizens, equilibrium tax-prices are given by

$$\frac{q_i}{a_{ij}} = \frac{U_{jSj}}{U_{jX_k}} \tag{A.22}$$

and the Pareto optimum by

$$\sum a_{ij}\frac{U_{jsj}}{U_{jXk}} = 1 \tag{A.23}$$

Similarly, if the problem was cast in terms of $f(a)$ instead of a, we would have

$$\frac{q_i}{f_{ij}(a_{ij})} = \frac{U_{jSj}}{U_{jXk}} \tag{A.24}$$

and

$$\sum f_{ij}(a_{ij}) \frac{U_{jSj}}{U_{jXk}} = 1 \tag{A.25}$$

The existence of non-private goods does not therefore alter the qualitative nature of the public goods problem, though it does change its quantitative significance. It is, therefore, legitimate at the analytical level to deal only with the case of pure public goods.

Appendix 2

The Long-Run Empirical Behavior
of Public Expenditures

Professors Peacock and Wiseman's empirical study[1] of the behavior of government expenditures in the United Kingdom covering the period between 1890 and 1955 provides an excellent focal point to discuss the large group of studies which are concerned with the secular behavior of aggregate government expenditures.[2] Though not supported by an econometric model such as the one developed by Davis, Dempster, and Wildavsky[3]

1. Peacock and Wiseman, *The Growth of Public Expenditure in the United Kingdom*.
2. R. A. Musgrave and J. M. Culbertson, "The Growth of Public Expenditures in the U.S., 1890–1948," *National Tax Journal* (June 1953), pp. 97–115; U. K. Hicks, *British Public Finances, 1880–1952* (London: Oxford University Press, 1954); M. S. Kendrick, *A Century and a Half of Federal Expenditure,* (New York: NBER, Occasional Paper no. 48, 1955); K. Emi, *Government Fiscal Activity and Economic Growth in Japan, 1868–1960,* (Tokyo: KINOKUNIYA Bookstore Co., Ltd., 1963); M. Copeland, *Trends in Government Financing* (Princeton: NBER, 1961); J. Veverka, "The Growth of Government Expenditure in the United Kingdom Since 1790," *Scottish Journal of Political Economy* (1963), pp. 111–27; S. Andic

(hereafter DDW), Peacock and Wiseman (PW) come to the conclusion, after a careful qualitative analysis of the data, that periods of fairly constant increases in expenditures, very much like what was recorded by DDW, are followed by important breaks or what they call "displacements" also much like what was observed by DDW. Johansen also confirmed the existence of "step-wise increases" in public expenditure after examining Norwegian data,[4] and a pattern roughly similar to the one portrayed in a stylized form in figure 11.1 appears to characterize the behavior of government expenditures in a large number of countries for which we possess data.

It is difficult to resist the idea that what Johansen calls "step-wise increases," what Peacock and Wiseman call "displacement effects," and what Davis, Dempster, and Wildavsky call "shift-points" all describe the same phenomenon, albeit at different levels of aggregation and with the use of different techniques; but the similarity of patterns is so great and seems so ubiquitous that I conclude the existence of a common underlying mechanism. Furthermore, Johansen's assertion seems very much

---

and J. Veverka, "The Growth of Government Expenditures in Germany Since the Unification," *Finanzarchiv* (January 1964) pp. 169–278; S. P. Gupta, "Public Expenditures and Economic Growth," *Public Finance* (Vol. 22, No. 4, 1967); A. Tait and M. O'Donoghue, "Public Expenditures in Ireland," in J. Bristol and A. Tait, *Economic Policy in Ireland* (Dublin: Institute of Public Administration, 1968); R. M. Bird, *The Growth of Government Spending in Canada* (Toronto: Canadian Tax Foundation, 1970). A number of the studies are summarized in R. A. Musgrave, *Fiscal Systems* (New Haven: Yale University Press, 1969).

3. O. A. Davis, M. A. H. Dempster, and A. Wildavsky, "On the Process of Budgeting: An Empirical Study of Congressional Appropriation;" also "A Theory of the Budgetary Process." See also chapter 9 above.

4. L. Johansen, *Public Economics* (Amsterdam: North Holland Publishing Co. 1965), chapter 6.

5. See note 4 above, p. 156.

to the point that if public expenditures were determined by a mechanism resembling Lindahl's exchange mechanism, or by one like that which underlies the social welfare function or the principles of logrolling, the pattern of government expenditure that would be observed would not display the step properties it now displays.[5] That fact had also been recognized by Peacock and Wiseman and by a number of other writers.

Though the product of similar forces, DDW's displacements are not likely to be observed at the same points as those of PW and of other researchers working in their tradition. The reason for this is simple. A displacement observed in one particular agency is not likely to produce any marked observable displacement in the series of total government expenditures, even if that displacement is fairly large and not compensated by a displacement of opposite size in another agency, unless, of course, the first agency itself accounts for a fairly large fraction of total public expenditures. Moreover, if a large displacement is completely or partially compensated by one of opposite sign in another department, aggregate behavior will hide the true pattern of public expenditures. It is for this reason that I believe DDW's results to be more reliable: disaggregation is less likely than aggregation to hide what is going on in the public sector; disaggregated analyses usually display many more shifts over a given period of time and thus will not induce us to formulate a theory or accept one that can only explain large displacements and thus, of necessity, let the smaller shifts go by.

Peacock and Wiseman's explanation of the step-wise increases in public expenditures can be summarized as follows: the ratio of public expenditure to G.N.P. (or the average real per capita level of public expenditures) desired by citizens is a magnitude that grows with the passage of time; that phenomenon may be related to changing tastes, or, with given tastes, to the existence of G.N.P. elasticity of the demand for public expenditure that is greater than one, a phenomenon which in turn may result from increasing externalities brought about by economic and population growth or by any other possible factor, but it is not really important to inquire into the causes of this desire for larger public spending. What is important is that this desired increase in public expenditures is not matched by an increase in revenue, because "notions about taxation are likely to be more influential than ideas about desirable increases in expenditure in deciding the size and rate of growth of the public sector" and "in settled times" these notions are not likely to change.[6] Indeed they will (only?) change with social upheavals, economic crises, war, and similar events, and with these changes revenues will be permitted to increase (or to fall) and actual public expenditures equalized to desired expenditures, giving rise to the observed displacement in the data.

In some ways this mechanism accounts for what is observed, but, as I understand it, it is not one that is easily rationalized or, to put it differently, it is not one for which a model firmly anchored in modern decision theory can be easily developed; indeed, note that the mechanism is not one of the private-demand-and-collective-supply type analyzed by Buchanan.[7] For if it was, it would be rooted in choice theory, but it is one that relies almost exclusively, but certainly essentially, on lags, thresholds, inertia, and habits. I am not saying that these factors do not have a role to play in the determination of government expenditures, but that role should, I think, be subordinate to choice and decision mechanisms and the consequent adjustment processes.

6. Peacock and Wiseman, *The Growth of Public Expenditure in the United Kingdom,* p. xxxiv.

7. J. M. Buchanan, "The Inconsistencies of the National Health Service," London: *Institute of Economic Affairs* (Occasional Paper no. 7, 1965).

The model put forward in this study does that. It has no difficulty in explaining why major social unheavals, economic crises, and wars, because they increase the level of coercion to which individuals are subjected, reduce the *relative* costs of political participation and, depending on the configuration of the other factors discussed in earlier chapters, can account for what is observed. It is capable, in addition, of being formulated in such a way as to provide an explanation for the much more numerous, but smaller, displacements which disaggregation reveals to be present in the data, displacements that are significant.

In conclusion, let me stress that the model developed in this book is not in contradiction to that of Peacock and Wiseman; indeed, it can be extended to incorporate such factors as lags, habits, and inertia, but being more general, it is capable of accounting for more.

Index